While There's Still Time

An Urgent Call To Pray For America

Joel R. Stroud

ISBN-13: 978-0-9973813-6-8

DEDICATION

In the early 1990's, Lucius Marion, revivalist and Pastor Emeritus of Clarksdale Baptist Church in Clarksdale, MS, asked me to commit to pray daily for revival in America. Although he went to be with our Lord Jesus in January of 2003, the memory of his challenge and example have encouraged me to become an intercessor for America. To the memory of my dear friend, this book is affectionately dedicated.

CONTENTS

ACKNOWLEDGMENTS

Special thanks is extended to my niece, Dr. April Roberts, for proof-reading the manuscript and to my brother, Daniel Stroud, Jr., for his many helpful suggestions. I am also very grateful to my wife, Sheri, for her insights, encouragement, and great cover design.

1- A Nation In Need Of Healing

If the foundations be destroyed, what can the righteous do...Ps. 11:3

1-1 Crumbling Foundations

Have you ever wondered what is happening in America? Do you sometimes remember better times and think, "How did we get into this mess?" Have you ever questioned why conditions are steadily deteriorating despite all of the money being invested in education, social programs, crime prevention, etc., in an attempt to solve our problems? More importantly, would you like to know what you can do to help stem the tide of evil engulfing our land?

We are in a national crisis. The building blocks of our society are slowly but steadily being dismantled and cast aside. The Bible, on which our government and legal system are based, and the Christian faith, that makes our form of government work, have been discarded as outdated and unreliable. Belief in the sanctity of human life that establishes the value of every individual, Christian morality that sustains an orderly society, and a Biblical work ethic that has prospered us beyond every other nation on the face of the earth are no longer the values of America.

In June of 2015, the Supreme Court of the United States held that the 14th Amendment to the U.S. Constitution required all states to grant and recognize same-sex marriages throughout America. Ignoring God's Word, the intent of our Founding Fathers, two hundred and thirty nine years of legal precedent, as well as thousands of years of human history, five of the nine Supreme Court justices decided that same sex marriage is a right guaranteed by the Constitution. In an unprecedented, but not unexpected ruling, the most fundamental institution of American society—marriage and family life—was redefined by judicial decree.

In light of these seismic, societal changes, many Christians have given up hope. Others remain hopefully optimistic while the question on everyone's heart is that raised by the psalmist...

> Psa. 11:3 If the foundations be destroyed, what can the righteous do?

If the building blocks of our society—the faith, values, institutions, and conventions on which America was established—are destroyed, what can the people of God do?

In the following pages I will lead you to discover the answer to that critical concern by posing and answering three questions based upon the following text. Thoroughly familiarize yourself with it for it holds the answer to our dilemma.

> 2 Chron. 7:12 Then the Lord appeared to Solomon by night, and said to him: "I have heard your prayer, and have chosen this place for Myself as a house of sacrifice.
> 2 Chron. 7:13 When I shut up heaven and there is no rain, or command the locusts to devour the land, or send pestilence among My people,
> 2 Chron. 7:14 <u>If My people who are called by My name will humble themselves, and pray and seek My</u>

face, and turn from their wicked ways, then I will hear from heaven, and will forgive their sin and heal their land.
2 Chron. 7:15 Now My eyes will be open and My ears attentive to prayer *made* in this place.
2 Chron. 7:16 For now I have chosen and sanctified this house, that My name may be there forever; and My eyes and My heart will be there perpetually.

1-2 Is America In Need Of Healing?

The concept of land being healed is based on the fact that under the Mosaic covenant, one of the principle ways God judged His people was by cursing the land. In Leviticus 26, God recorded for every generation of His people the chastisements they could expect for disregarding His holy Law.

> Lev. 26:20 And your strength shall be spent in vain; for your land shall not yield its produce, nor shall the trees of the land yield their fruit.
>
> Lev. 26:32 I will bring the land to desolation, and your enemies who dwell in it shall be astonished at it.
> Lev. 26:33 I will scatter you among the nations and draw out a sword after you; your land shall be desolate and your cities waste.
> Lev. 26:34 Then the land shall enjoy its sabbaths as long as it lies desolate and you *are* in your enemies' land; then the land shall rest and enjoy its sabbaths.
> Lev. 26:35 As long as *it* lies desolate it shall rest—for the time it did not rest on your sabbaths when you dwelt in it.

Crop failures, the desolation of the land, enemy invasions, and ultimately, exile among the nations were judgments God promised His people for disobeying His commandments.

Based on a literal reading of these verses, some might argue that our land is not in need of healing. We continue to enjoy abundant rainfall, and our land yields plentiful crops. Our cities are the most modern, best maintained, and most secure in the world. Among the nations, America ranks at or near the top in every metric—health care, economic strength, education, transportation, communication, etc. Our enemies have not overrun us, destroyed our cities, and left us as refugees among the nations. Sure, we have our share of problems, but for the most part, things are not so bad "in the land of the free and the home of the brave."

However, this "head in the sand" view of American life completely misses the shocking moral and spiritual problems that confront our nation, reflected in the epidemic of recreational sex, drug abuse, pornography, gang involvement, violent crime, human trafficking, suicide, prostitution, identity theft, and acts of murder and mayhem in our streets, schools, malls, and public places. Abortion continues to snuff out the lives of the unborn, now numbering more than sixty million. Divorce is epidemic with 50% of marriages failing and more couples choosing to live together rather than marry. X, XX, XXX rated entertainment and video games allow young and old to immerse themselves in a virtual world of crime, sex, and violence. Undeniably, we are awash in a sea of moral sewage that is desensitizing us to evil and poisoning our souls.

In 2015, secretly recorded videotapes unmasked Planned Parenthood officials freely discussing the killing of babies in the womb and the sale of their body parts for profit. Subsequently, the only persons charged with criminal behavior in the matter were those who exposed the barbaric and inhuman enterprise.

If that were not enough to show how desensitized and confused our society has become, consider this: At last count, the admissions application used by the University of California gave prospective students six options to indicate their gender. They may choose traditional categories of male and female or trans male, trans female, gender non-conforming, and different identity.

America is sick, but not like someone in the hospital hooked up to IV's, being pumped with antibiotics to kill the infection.

Such a person is sick, but he is getting the needed treatment. He has a good chance of recovery if he follow the doctor's orders. However, that is not how America is sick. Our nation is like an apparently healthy person walking around with a rapidly growing, yet undiagnosed cancer that has already spread to other organs of the body. We are deathly ill. We just don't know it, yet. Furthermore, if something does not happen soon, when we finally realize how sick we are, it will be too late.

Tragically, the vast majority of Americans are oblivious to the danger facing us. They look to Washington or to so-called experts who are supposed to understand the political, social, and moral issues we face. Yet, modern experts have no lasting solutions because they do not believe God. They refuse to consult the only book that has the correct answers.

At times, pastors have been accused of being too negative and preaching doom and gloom, but hear me clearly: America is not too big to fail! We need spiritual healing in our land. Without it, we will die. We also need a spiritual house cleaning in the church. Without it, we cannot lead this nation to spiritual awakening.

1-3 Judgment: Remedial Or Ultimate

Many factors have contributed to the rapid decline of American society over the past 75 years. Some would point to our long history of oppressing and exploiting minorities and resisting efforts that would have granted the promise of "liberty and justice for all" guaranteed by our constitution.

Others could point to the negative impact of World War II when wives and mothers left the home to join the work force while their men were away at war. That was certainly the beginning of powerful social changes that negatively impacted family life. The pattern of the "breadwinner husband" and the "stay at home mom" slowly began to erode and undermine the traditional family.

There are those who might point to the 1950's when the middle class of America began to prosper and Rock and Roll took the country by storm. Rebellion came into vogue among the youth, and economic prosperity caused many Americans to forget the God who had given it. A similar economic boom is currently happening among many minorities, and we should be praying they do not fall victim to the deceitfulness of riches.

Some would trace our problems to the 60's and the anti-war movement, the drug culture, the outlawing of prayer and Bible reading in our schools, the advent of cheap birth control, and the resulting sexual revolution that swept across our college campuses.

Those of us who grew up in the 70's could point to the infamous Supreme Court decision that declared war on the unborn as a cause for America's rapid decline. These were all significant developments that forever changed generations of Americans, but they were more symptoms of a deeper problem than actual causes.

There is no question these factors were powerful catalysts for change and produced watershed moments in our history. However, no single factor can explain our moral and spiritual decline. Rather, it has been a combination of numerous collective decisions, governmental actions, legal rulings, and corporate behaviors that has slowly brought America into disfavor with Almighty God. Nevertheless, all of our national offenses can be boiled down to one fundamental issue: We have deliberately and defiantly turned our backs on the God who made us great and rejected the Bible as the authority for our lives. This we have done, and the cost has been immeasurable!

It is equally clear from the Scriptures that the judgment of God awaits those nations and civilizations that refuse to acknowledge His glory and reject His Word. Do not be deceived: God will not let America or any other nation go unpunished. Notice the sober warning of coming judgment recorded in the Scriptures.

> Ps. 9:17 The wicked shall be turned into hell, and all the nations that forget God.

Therefore, how does God judge nations? He does so in two basic ways—through remedial discipline and ultimate destruction. Remedial discipline occurs when God withholds blessings to chastise a nation and bring it to repentance, illustrated by the following account from the book of Judges.

> Judges 6:11 Now the Angel of the Lord came and sat under the terebinth tree which *was* in Ophrah, which *belonged* to Joash the Abiezrite, while his son Gideon threshed wheat in the winepress, in order to hide *it* from the Midianites.
> Judges 6:12 And the Angel of the Lord appeared to him, and said to him, "The Lord is with you, you mighty man of valor!"
> Judges 6:13 Gideon said to Him, "O my lord, if the Lord is with us, why then has all this happened to us? And where *are* all His miracles which our fathers told us about, saying, 'Did not the Lord bring us up from Egypt?' But now the Lord has forsaken us and delivered us into the hands of the Midianites."

God's remedial judgment came in the form of Midianite incursions to discipline His people and motivate them to repent and cry out for deliverance. On the other hand, ultimate judgment is when God says, "Enough is enough!" and destroys a nation. Mind you, it only happens after repeated refusal of His remedial discipline, but when it finally comes, there is no escape. In the book of Proverbs, the wisdom of God teaches us…

> Pro. 29:1 He who is often rebuked, *and* hardens *his* neck, will suddenly be destroyed, and that without remedy.

Moreover, what is true of individuals is also true of nations. God has a spiritual barometer, a sin meter, for the nations. When the Amorite civilization had reached the point of no return, God decreed destruction and used the Israelites to affect it upon their deliverance from Egypt and conquest of Canaan.

> Gen. 15:15 "Now as for you, you shall go to your fathers in peace; you shall be buried at a good old age.

> Gen. 15:16 But in the fourth generation they shall return here, for the iniquity of the Amorites *is* not yet complete (full)."

If America continues to refuse God's correction, our iniquity will come to the full and the Lord will decree destruction. In the days of Jeremiah, Israel had reached such a point, and even the prayers of God's prophet could not avert judgment.

> Jer. 7:13 And now, because you have done all these works," says the Lord, "and I spoke to you, rising up early and speaking, but you did not hear, and I called you, but you did not answer,
> Jer. 7:14 Therefore I will do to the house which is called by My name, in which you trust, and to this place which I gave to you and your fathers, as I have done to Shiloh.
> Jer. 7:15 And I will cast you out of My sight, as I have cast out all your brethren—the whole posterity of Ephraim.
> Jer. 7:16 "Therefore do not pray for this people, nor lift up a cry or prayer for them, nor make intercession to Me; for I will not hear you.

1-4 The Process Of Reprobation

There is another aspect of divine judgment that often goes unnoticed. God's judgment involves nations and cultures being *progressively* given up to their own wicked desires because they refuse to acknowledge their Creator. This process is called *reprobation.* Romans 1 clearly describes the process of gradual reprobation that overtakes nations that reject the knowledge of God. Notice the following verses.

> Rom. 1:21 Because, although they knew God, they did not glorify *Him* as God, nor were thankful, but became futile in their thoughts, and their foolish hearts were darkened.

> Rom. 1:22 Professing to be wise, they became fools,
> Rom. 1:23 And changed the glory of the incorruptible God into an image made like corruptible man—and birds and four-footed animals and creeping things.
> Rom. 1:24 Therefore God also gave them up to uncleanness, in the lusts of their hearts, to dishonor their bodies among themselves,
> Rom. 1:25 Who exchanged the truth of God for the lie, and worshiped and served the creature rather than the Creator, who is blessed forever. Amen.
> Rom. 1:26 For this reason God gave them up to vile passions. For even their women exchanged the natural use for what is against nature.
> Rom. 1:27 Likewise also the men, leaving the natural use of the woman, burned in their lust for one another, men with men committing what is shameful, and receiving in themselves the penalty of their error which was due.
> Rom. 1:28 And even as they did not like to retain God in *their* knowledge, God gave them over to a reprobate mind, to do those things which are not fitting;

Three times the Scriptures record that God gave them up. The text does not say *He gave up on them*, but *He gave them up* to progressively deeper levels of sin and depravity. Following are a few examples of how this has worked out in our national life:

- We reject God's glory; He gives us up to false religions.

- We reject God's moral absolutes; He gives us over to situational ethics and moral relativism.

- We reject God's record of creation; He gives us over to the lie of evolution.

- We reject God's standards for sexual expression; He gives us up to immorality and perversion.

- We reject God's wisdom regarding money management; He gives us over to debt and the sting of high interest.

- We reject God's standards of just punishment; He gives us up to rampant crime.

- We reject God's standard of the sanctity of life; He gives us over to abortion and euthanasia or so-called mercy killing.

- We reject God's standard of parenting and child rearing; He gives us up to juvenile crime, teen pregnancy, gang involvement, and addictions of all kinds. Incidentally, it was George Washington, our first president, who warned, "The future of our nation depends upon the *Christian* training of our children."

- We reject God's standard of marriage (one man and one woman for life); He gives us up to divorce, cohabitation, civil unions, and same sex marriage.

- We reject the God ordained roles and responsibilities of husbands and wives; He gives us up to dysfunctional families where fathers are absent and husbands live with their wives in a state of estrangement while children are left to raise themselves.

- We reject God's standards of neighbor love and justice; He gives us up to oppression and racism.

For many years, preachers have been warning their congregations that God would judge America if we did not repent. The truth is God has already been judging America because we have not repented. That is why things have steadily gone from bad to worse. We have rejected God and the Bible, and He has given us up to deeper and deeper levels of spiritual and moral reprobation. It did not happen all at once, but slowly, steadily, at times almost imperceptibly, our beliefs and values have changed, and we have ceased to be a Christian nation. That is how we have come to this moment.

1-5 How Can Healing Occur?

2 Chronicles 7:14 is a promise to the nation of Israel, but it reveals the principles that are necessary for God to heal any nation.

> 2 Chron. 7:14 If My people who are called by My name will humble themselves, and pray and seek My face, and turn from their wicked ways, then I will hear from heaven, and will forgive their sin and heal their land.

Five actions are necessary. The first is implied while the other four are stated. Memorize them, meditate on them, and obey them.

1) We must acknowledge and take responsibility for the problem.
2) We must humble ourselves in the sight of God.
3) We must pray as we have never prayed before.
4) We must seek God's face.
5) We must turn from our wicked ways.

I know this is not what Christians want to hear, but the problem with our nation is not with the lost, but with the saved. God said, "If *my people*, who are called by *my name…*" I love God's people. I believe they are the best thing about America. However, the solution to our nation's problems does not lie with sinners, but with saints. America's hope does not lie in the White House or the courthouse, but in the church house. Judgment must begin at the house of God, or revival and awakening will not come to our land. Healing for America is possible, but it will require something of you and me. *We* must obey the principles of 2 Chronicles 7:14.

First, we must take responsibility for the state of our families, our churches, and our nation and stop blaming sinners for our troubles. God is not waiting for pimps, prostitutes, perverts, gang-bangers, crooked politicians, and the Hollywood crowd to repent. He is waiting for us, those who are called by His name, to return to Him.

Second, we must demonstrate genuine humility and reject our prideful independence. God resists the proud but gives grace to the humble. Pride will keep a person from Christ, and it will keep God's people from revival. We must recognize and reject pride in any and every form. We must own our sin and agree in our hearts with the words of the old spiritual,

> "It's not my brother or my sister but it's me,
> O Lord, standing in the need of prayer."

Third, we must quit saying prayers and begin to call on God in fervent, believing prayer. Jesus said, "My Father's house shall be called a house of prayer…" Our churches have become houses of everything but prayer. Many feel more like nightclubs than sanctuaries and are more about entertainment than worship in spirit and truth. However, if we would experience revival, we must turn our churches into houses of prayer. As Leonard Ravenhill asserted, "We must pray alone; we must pray together; we must pray in the night and not cease in the day…We must engage in protracted prayer, groaning prayer, fasting prayer, and weeping prayer." We must be like wrestling Jacob who would not let God go until He blessed him. We must become watchmen upon the walls who will not give God rest day or night until He establishes His glory in His church.

Fourth, we must seek God's face, not His hand. We must desire God for His own sake, not for His blessings. We must get to know and rejoice in Him, not just be concerned with what He can give us. We must seek to please Him and not ourselves or others. We must learn to live in His presence, for in His presence is fullness of joy and at His right hand are pleasures forever more.

Fifth, we must turn from our wicked ways—ways that seem right to us but lead to death—and learn to walk in the ways of God. ***Our ways*** are the typical manner in which we respond to daily issues, especially when we are under pressure. We must replace ***our ways*** of self-exaltation with self-denial, deception with truth, compromise with integrity, self-justification with humble confession, carnality with spirituality, fearfulness with courage, self-confidence with dependence on God, etc.

What I have shared is a tall order, and it won't be easy. But we cannot continue to hide our head in the sand and hope things will get better. We cannot continue business as usual and escape the judgment of God. We must lead our families, churches, and communities to return to the Lord. Better education, more jobs, and higher salaries alone will not stop the decline of our cities and our nation. Without the spiritual and moral transformation that results from a personal relationship with Jesus Christ, we, our children, and our nation have no hope.

1-6 Needed: Intercessors

In describing the forces that joined the ranks of David's army, the Bible states...

> 1 Chron. 12:32 Of the sons of Issachar who had understanding of the times, to know what Israel ought to do, their chiefs were two hundred; and all their brethren were at their command;

Not every soldier from the tribes of Israel was like these two hundred of the tribe of Issachar. They were special, and they were given authority to lead. Why? Because they "had understanding of the times" and because they knew "what Israel ought to do."

Many believers see the problems we face and can discern their cause. However, not as many know how to respond. We spend a lot of time complaining about the issues and blaming those we feel are responsible, but very little time doing anything to make a difference. Oswald Chambers provides the following helpful comments in his excellent devotional, *My Utmost For His Highest*: "We see where other folks are failing, and we turn our discernment into the gibe of criticism instead of into intercession on their behalf...Discernment is God's call to intercession, never to fault finding" (3/31, 5/3).

Like it or not, Christians are the conscience of America, and it is time we began to speak up and let our voice be heard. We must raise the alarm and call God's people to pray and seek His face. We must become catalysts for revival in our churches by seeking God and encouraging others to do the same. We must become prayer warriors standing in the gap for our families, our churches, and our nation.

It may surprise you, but according to God's Word, ultimate judgment will not fall on America because of the wickedness of unbelievers. It will be due to the apathy and unbelief of Christians. One of the saddest statements in all the Bible is found in the book of Ezekiel.

> Eze. 22:30 So I sought for a man among them who would make a wall, and stand in the gap before Me on behalf of the land, that I should not destroy it; but I found no one.
> Eze. 22:31 Therefore I have poured out My indignation on them; I have consumed them with the fire of My wrath; and I have recompensed their deeds on their own heads," says the Lord GOD.

In the days of Ezekiel, God looked for an intercessor, someone who believed God and shared His concerns. He searched for someone to stay His wrath by standing in the gap and making up the hedge. God was looking for prayer warriors who would stand as one man to intercede for the nation, but *He found none*. Consequently, He poured out His indignation and consumed them in His wrath. National judgment finally fell not simply due to the wickedness of the wicked but because of the failure of the righteous. There was no intercessor—no one to stand in the gap.

Edmund Burke, a noted Irish political philosopher and statesman who is often regarded as the father of modern conservatism, once said, "All that is necessary for the triumph of evil is that good men do nothing." What we need today are men and women of understanding who know what we ought to do and are willing to do it. With God's help, would you be that person?

- Would you let God break your heart with the things that break His heart?

- Would you give yourself as an intercessor to stand in the gap and make up the hedge around your family, church, community, and nation?

- Would you pray daily for the salvation of your leaders and for all those in authority?

- Would you pray for the lost and for those who were once faithful?

- Would you pray daily for revival and spiritual awakening in America?

- With God's help, would you be an intercessor for America?

The future of our families, our churches, and generations of Americans depends on how we respond to God's call.

2- Disasters: Why?

Unless you repent, you will all likewise perish...Luke 13:5

2-1 The Need For Repentance

Hurricane Harvey was the first major hurricane of the 2017 Atlantic Hurricane Season. In a period of four days, Harvey dumped as much as 52 inches of rain on Houston and the surrounding area, causing unprecedented flooding and becoming "the wettest tropical cyclone on record in the contiguous United States." Floodwaters inundated hundreds of thousands of homes, displaced tens of thousands of Texans, and prompted more than 17,000 rescues.

Harvey began as a tropical wave and intensified into a Category 4 hurricane on August 24, making landfall near Rockport, Texas. The hurricane caused at least 70 confirmed deaths and catastrophic flooding in the greater Houston metropolitan area. Experts called Harvey the worst disaster in Texas history and projected the recovery would take many years.

Preliminary estimates of economic and property loss ran as high as $190 billion, the most from a storm in US history.

So, why did Harvey happen? What lesson should we take from this and other disasters. More importantly, what is God's take on the growing number of calamities that have befallen America in recent years? In this chapter, I will help you think God's thoughts about disasters and discern what He is saying to us and our leaders. Consider the following passage.

> Luke 13:1 There were present at that season some who told Him about the Galileans whose blood Pilate had mingled with their sacrifices.
> Luke 13:2 And Jesus answered and said to them, "Do you suppose that these Galileans were worse sinners than all *other* Galileans, because they suffered such things?
> Luke 13:3 I tell you, no; but unless you repent you will all likewise perish.
> Luke 13:4 Or those eighteen on whom the tower in Siloam fell and killed them, do you think that they were worse sinners than all *other* men who dwelt in Jerusalem?
> Luke 13:5 I tell you, no; but unless you repent you will all likewise perish."
> Luke 13:6 He also spoke this parable: "A certain *man* had a fig tree planted in his vineyard, and he came seeking fruit on it and found none.
> Luke 13:7 Then he said to the keeper of his vineyard, 'Look, for three years I have come seeking fruit on this fig tree and find none. Cut it down; why does it use up the ground?'
> Luke 13:8 But he answered and said to him, 'Sir, let it alone this year also, until I dig around it and fertilize *it*.
> Luke 13:9 And if it bears fruit, *well*. But if not, after that you can cut it down.'"

In these verses, Jesus spoke directly to the issue of disasters. Read them carefully, and ask the Lord to open your ears to what He is saying to America.

2-2 Missing The Message

Jesus' teaching on the significance of disasters was prompted when some in His audience mentioned a well-known calamity that had befallen some of their countrymen.

> Luke 13:1 There were present at that season some who told Him about the Galileans whose blood Pilate had mingled with their sacrifices.

The first tragedy Jesus addressed befell a group of Galileans. Though not as scorned as Samaritans, they were generally regarded with contempt by the more sophisticated, religious folks of Jerusalem.

In many ways, Galilee was a dark place. Matthew recorded the prophecy of Isaiah, describing the pagan influence and spiritual darkness that would be there when the Messiah arrived (Isa. 9:1-2).

> Mt. 4:15 "The land of Zebulun and the land of Naphtali, by the way of the sea, beyond the Jordan, Galilee of the Gentiles:
> Mt. 4:16 The people who sat in darkness have seen a great light, and upon those who sat in the region and shadow of death Light has dawned."

The Galileans in question were at the temple to worship. The reason Pilate ordered their execution is unknown, but the Romans were very brutal when dealing with any actions that challenged their authority. In any event, the blood of the Galileans was mingled with the blood of the sacrifices they had offered to God. In some ways, it was not unlike the tragic and deplorable murder of twenty six members of the First Baptist Church of Sutherland Springs, TX in November of 2017.

The second calamity Jesus mentioned was more like a natural disaster.

> Luke 13:4 Or those eighteen on whom the tower in Siloam fell and killed them, do you think that they

> were worse sinners than all *other* men who dwelt in Jerusalem?

A tower in Jerusalem had collapsed killing eighteen people. Whether the result of faulty construction, erosion of the foundation, an earthquake, or some other cause is not known, but it seemed to be a natural and unexpected disaster—what we once called an act of God. In any case, the religious folks had an explanation for why this event and the atrocity involving the Galileans had occurred. Discerning the pride, prejudice, and blindness of their hearts, Jesus seized the opportunity to correct their wrong way of thinking.

The prevailing notion among the Jewish leaders and the people generally was that all who suffered great calamity must surely be great sinners, and the worse the affliction, the more it must have been deserved. The disciples expressed this opinion in connection with the man who had been born blind in John 9.

> John 9:1 Now as *Jesus* passed by, He saw a man who was blind from birth.
> John 9:2 And His disciples asked Him, saying, "Rabbi, who sinned, this man or his parents, that he was born blind?"

Like others, they thought this man's suffering was because he or his parents had done something bad. Today, we sometimes hear similar suggestions from charismatics, faith healers, and positive thinking gurus who teach that if you are not healthy, wealthy, and enjoying "your best life now," the fault is with you. There must be something wrong with your faith. There must be sin in your life.

However, Jesus said, "no" to the nonsense of the disciples and gave a reason for the man's malady which they had never considered.

> John 9:3 Jesus answered, "Neither this man nor his parents sinned, but that the works of God should be revealed in him.

According to Jesus, all sickness and suffering are not the direct result of sin. Some are, but some are not. If you drink until you get cirrhosis of the liver, you can blame that on sin. If you are diagnosed with cancer after smoking for years, you can attribute that to sin. If you live to be ninety-nine and finally just wear out, you can say that is also the result of sin since physical death is the result of Adam's disobedience and the effects of sin working in his children. However, sometimes people are afflicted through no fault of their own, even with birth defects, that the works of God may be revealed in them.

2-3 A Solemn Warning

Using the calamities of the Galileans, Jesus posed a question to His audience.

> Luke 13:2 And Jesus answered and said to them, "Do you suppose that these Galileans were worse sinners than all *other* Galileans, because they suffered such things?

In effect, our Lord asked, "What do you think is the meaning of this calamity? Do you really believe the Galileans who perished were greater sinners than all other Galileans? Did the circumstances of their death—murdered while they were worshipping God—mean they deserved to die that way?"

Jesus' question probably surprised His listeners. Had they been given opportunity to defend their position, they might have said, "Well, of course they were great sinners. Haven't you heard of the flood in Noah's day and the story of Sodom and Gomorrah?" They might have cited Proverbs 6 to support their belief.

> Pro. 6:12 A worthless person, a wicked man, walks with a perverse mouth;
> Pro. 6:13 He winks with his eyes, he shuffles his feet, he points with his fingers;
> Pro. 6:14 Perversity *is* in his heart, he devises evil

> continually, he sows discord.
> Pro. 6:15 Therefore his calamity shall come suddenly; suddenly he shall be broken without remedy.

Nevertheless, Jesus told them, "You're looking at this all wrong, and you are missing what God is saying to you."

> Luke 13:3 I tell you, no; but unless you repent you will all likewise perish.

Then He followed up with a similar question about the tower that collapsed in Jerusalem.

> Luke 13:4 Or those eighteen on whom the tower in Siloam fell and killed them, do you think that they were worse sinners than all *other* men who dwelt in Jerusalem?
> Luke 13:5 I tell you, no; but unless you repent you will all likewise perish."

It is important not to misunderstand what Jesus said. He did not deny that God judges sin with calamity. He did not deny that sometimes great suffering may be because of great sin. He did not deny that the Galileans were sinners deserving God's judgment. He did not even deny those eighteen men who were crushed by the tower were sinners deserving God's wrath. However, what He did deny was that their suffering was because they were worse sinners than anyone else—worse sinners say, than His hearers or than you and me.

After correcting the mistaken notion that calamity only befalls the greatest of sinners, Jesus issued a remarkable warning to His listeners. He repeated it so there would be no mistake.

> Luke 13:3 I tell you, no; but unless you repent you will all likewise perish.

> Luke 13:5 I tell you, no; but unless you repent you will all likewise perish."

Jesus told His audience that if they refused to repent they would die in a similar manner as the Galileans and the men of Jerusalem.

Surely these statements must have shocked the crowd. They did not feel they had any need of repentance. They believed bad things only happened to bad people. Nothing bad had happened to them, so that meant they were okay. These good, religious folks did not feel they were great sinners. Like us, they probably talked about how horrific the calamity was, how tragic for the families of those who perished, how long it would take them to get over it, and how much money would be required to rebuild the tower. Perhaps, some of them gave money to help the families of those who died or volunteered to help clear away the rubble of the collapsed tower, but all the while they felt okay about themselves. In fact, down deep they felt a little superior to those who had perished.

Nevertheless, Jesus' warning forced His audience to realize the disasters that had befallen their countrymen were not just tragic events of the past. The lesson of calamity was for the living, not the dead. The dead were gone. It was too late for them, but the living still had time. His listeners could still learn from what had happened.

> Luke 13:3 I tell you, no; but unless you repent you will all likewise perish.

Jesus said, "I am telling ***you***. ***You*** are no better than they were. ***You*** must repent, or a similar fate awaits ***you***."

These calamities were in the past, but they had meaning for the *present* as well as the *future*.

> Luke 13:3 I tell you, no; but unless you repent (now) you will (future) all likewise perish.

Jesus warned the people, "You must act now; you must repent today. If you fail to turn from your sins now, in the future you will die as tragically as these have died." In reality, Jesus was offering them an opportunity to avoid impending judgment.

2-4 Exiles Among The Nations

Our Lord knew that in a short time, He would be rejected by the nation and crucified. In Matthew 20, He told His disciples,

> Mt. 20:18 "Behold, we are going up to Jerusalem, and the Son of Man will be betrayed to the chief priests and to the scribes; and they will condemn Him to death,
> Mt. 20:19 And deliver Him to the Gentiles to mock and to scourge and to crucify. And the third day He will rise again."

Jesus knew that those who believed Him and heeded His warning would be delivered from the catastrophic judgment that was about to come on the Jewish nation.

In Luke 21, Jesus prophesied of Jerusalem's destruction in AD 70, just forty years in the future.

> Luke 21:20 "But when you see Jerusalem surrounded by armies, then know that its desolation is near.

He went on to warn the Jews to flee to the mountains to escape the coming conflagration, which many did in AD 66 following the surprising retreat of the Romans under the command of the Syrian Legate, Cestius Gallus.

> Luke 21:21 Then let those who are in Judea flee to the mountains, let those who are in the midst of her depart, and let not those who are in the country enter her.

In his history of the Jews, Josephus recorded that following the defeat of Cestius at the hand of the Jewish defenders, many of the citizens of Jerusalem left the city as from a sinking ship.

As a prophet of God, Jesus not only warned those who would listen, He also foretold the suffering that would befall those who refused to believe His words.

> Luke 21:22 For these are the days of vengeance, that all things which are written may be fulfilled.
> Luke 21:23 But woe to those who are pregnant and to those who are nursing babies in those days! For there will be great distress in the land and wrath upon this people.
> Luke 21:24 And they will fall by the edge of the sword, and be led away captive into all nations. And Jerusalem will be trampled by Gentiles until the times of the Gentiles are fulfilled.

Four years after the humiliating defeat of Cestius Gallus, the Roman General, Titus, returned to Jerusalem and laid siege to the city again, but this time there was no opportunity to escape. In the ensuing holocaust, one million, one hundred thousand Jews perished, and the rest were sold as slaves and scattered throughout the Roman Empire just as Jesus had predicted.

In His warning to repent, Jesus was saying, "While there's still time, wake up. Learn from the calamity that has happened to others. Just because you have avoided calamity doesn't mean you have no need of repentance." Israel was under national judgment, and it could only be averted by corporate or national repentance.

Following His sober warning, Jesus concluded His discourse with a parable.

> Luke 13:6 He also spoke this parable: "A certain *man* had a fig tree planted in his vineyard, and he came seeking fruit on it and found none.
> Luke 13:7 Then he said to the keeper of his vineyard, 'Look, for three years I have come seeking fruit on this fig tree and find none. Cut it down; why does it use up the ground?'
> Luke 13:8 But he answered and said to him, 'Sir, let it alone this year also, until I dig around it and fertilize *it*.
> Luke 13:9 And if it bears fruit, *well*. But if not, after that you can cut it down.'"

In the parable the *certain man* represented God. He had created the nation and formed it for His glory. He desired them to be a holy people and a "light to the nations."

The *fig tree* represented the nation of Israel. They were to bring forth the fruit of love and obedience, but they were rebellious and stiff-necked. For a final three years, God had literally come to Israel in the person of Jesus Christ, calling them to become the people He desired them to be. However, their privileged position had produced pride, and their enlightenment had become blindness.

The *dresser of the vineyard* was Jesus. Like Moses, He stood as an intercessor and mediator between God and Israel. He pled with God for Israel and with Israel for God. He prayed, "Give them a little more time, let me cultivate and fertilize your fig tree, and then, if there is no fruit, cut it down."

History reveals that God did exactly that. Rather than receive Jesus' words, Israel rejected and crucified their Messiah and King. His attempts to cultivate and fertilize the fig tree were met with resistance and unbelief, so God used the Romans to destroy their temple and send His chosen people into exile among the nations.

2-5 Connecting The Dots

What does all this mean for us today? In light of the teaching of Jesus, I believe we can conclude the calamities of recent memory are God's wake-up calls to America. The tragic events of 9-11, the economic collapse of 2008, storms, fires, floods, chaos in our streets, mass shootings, and a historic pandemic are wake-up calls for you and me.

We feel spiritually and morally superior to the other nations of the world, but the truth is America is spiritually and morally reprobate. We have become deaf and blind to God's reproofs even though they are increasing in intensity and frequency.

The fourth stanza of our hymn "America The Beautiful" declares,

"Thine alabaster cities gleam,
Undimmed by human tears!"

This is no longer true. New York, the largest city in the US was hit by terrorists on September 11, 2001. Hurricane Katrina ravaged the cities of Florida and the Gulf Coast in 2005. In 2012 Super Storm Sandy devastated cities of the Atlantic coast from Florida to Maine. Harvey decimated the 4th largest city in the US. Just a short time later, Irma wreaked havoc all across Florida, and many are still mourning the calamity in Las Vegas. At the time of this writing, we are dealing with a deadly pandemic that has killed more than ninety thousand Americans, and the death toll is rising daily. The Coronavirus has shut down the economy of America and the world. Is anyone paying attention? Is anyone connecting the dots?

In Leviticus 26 and Deuteronomy 28, God promised disasters increasing in frequency and intensity to discipline Israel for their rebellion against His commandments, and we observe a similar pattern in God's dealing with America. Just as surely as the collapse of the tower of Siloam and the butchering of the Galileans were wake-up calls to Israel, disasters are God's wake-up calls to us. Calamities are the Lord's summons to repent.

Many who were familiar with the disasters of which Jesus spoke and heard His ominous words refused to listen, and they perished. About forty years after Jesus gave this warning to repent, the Romans laid siege to Jerusalem during the season of Passover. The city was packed with holiday pilgrims, and in the ensuing catastrophe, over a million Jews died by famine, crucifixion, and sword. An eyewitness account of the calamity written by Flavius Josephus can be found in his history entitled, *The Jewish War*.

When national judgment falls, it usually affects everyone just as it did in the days of Daniel. He and his companions, Hananiah,

Mishael, and Azariah, were godly young men, but they were gathered up with the other captives and carried off to Babylon. In corporate judgment, the righteous suffer with the wicked, and the children suffer for the sins of their fathers.

> Dan. 9:16 "O Lord, according to all Your righteousness, I pray, let Your anger and Your fury be turned away from Your city Jerusalem, Your holy mountain; because for our sins, and for the iniquities of our fathers, Jerusalem and Your people *are* a reproach to all *those* around us.

God does not hold anyone *personally* accountable for the sins of another.

> Deut. 24:16 "Fathers shall not be put to death for *their* children, nor shall children be put to death for *their* fathers; a person shall be put to death for his own sin.

However, when national (corporate) judgment falls, God visits the iniquities of the past on those living in the present. The children suffer for the sins of their fathers.

> Mt. 23:32 Fill up, then, the measure of your fathers' *guilt.*
> Mt. 23:33 Serpents, brood of vipers! How can you escape the condemnation of hell?
> Mt. 23:34 Therefore, indeed, I send you prophets, wise men, and scribes: *some* of them you will kill and crucify, and *some* of them you will scourge in your synagogues and persecute from city to city,
> Mt. 23:35 That on you may come all the righteous blood shed on the earth, from the blood of righteous Abel to the blood of Zechariah, son of Berechiah, whom you murdered between the temple and the altar.
> Mt. 23:36 Assuredly, I say to you, all these things will come upon this generation.

The same is true for us today. When God judges America, He will sum up the iniquity of past generations, and we will not escape.

2-6 Repent Or Perish!

Over the past several decades, America has experienced increasingly greater calamities, and we have not yet returned to the Lord. What will it take to wake us up? More hurricanes, another earthquake, only greater and in closer proximity to us or our loved ones? Maybe a missile from a rogue nuclear power or a dirty bomb smuggled within our borders and detonated near a major city? Perhaps another pandemic more deadly than Coronavirus—who knows? I do not claim to be a prophet, and I do not know what the future will bring, but I can assure you if we do not repent, we shall perish.

God established this nation. He has planted churches across America and blessed us with the choicest blessings of Heaven. He has been coming for years looking for and desiring fruit from our lives, but we have repaid Him with everything but love and obedience. We have not stood in the gap and interceded for America. We have not cultivated her soil with our supplications, fertilized her roots with our prayers and watered her leaves with our tears. We have not pled with God for our neighbors and pled with our neighbors for God. Instead, we have presumed on His goodness, taken advantage of His mercy, and disregarded His reproofs.

Stop and think for a moment. How did your life change as a result of 9/11? What impact did the economic collapse of 2008 have on your faithfulness? How did Katrina, Sandy, Harvey, and Irma affect your love and obedience to God? When it is no longer a threat, how will the Coronavirus affect your daily walk with Jesus, your church attendance, your service, your giving, and your witness to the lost? In the aftermath of 9-11, churches were filled because God had our attention, but we soon got over it. Now, we hardly give Him a second thought. And church? Well, who needs that?

You and I are no better than anyone else. Somehow we think if we have not raped, murdered, molested a child, or embezzled thousands of dollars, we are not worthy of judgment. However, the truth is "all have sinned and come short of the glory of God," and great or small, "the wages of sin is death." If we received what we deserved, we would have perished the first time we entertained an evil thought, told a lie, or mistreated someone.

Lamenting God's judgment upon his people at the hand of the Babylonians, Jeremiah found insight and hope when he considered the mercy of the Lord.

> Lam. 3:22 Through the Lord's mercies we are not consumed, because His compassions fail not.
> Lam. 3:23 They are new every morning; great is Your faithfulness.

Do not be deceived. The only reason you and I have not experienced calamitous judgment is because of the mercy of God, not because we have no need of repentance.

Each time disaster strikes, our leaders urge unity and tell us we will rebuild, we will recover, and we will be stronger than ever, and that sounds great. However, it completely misses the point because it leaves God out of the discussion. It is not climate change, Islamic Jihad, earthquakes, economic disasters, or pandemics we need to fear. It is the LORD God!

The Scriptures teach us that God is sovereign. He controls all things.

> Pro. 30:4 Who has ascended into heaven, or descended? Who has gathered the wind in His fists? Who has bound the waters in a garment? Who has established all the ends of the earth? What *is* His name, and what *is* His Son's name, if you know?

He rules the nations and determines their leaders.

> Dan. 4:17 'This decision *is* by the decree of the watchers, and the sentence by the word of the holy ones, in order that the living may know that the Most

> High rules in the kingdom of men, gives it to whomever He will, and sets over it the lowest of men.'

The Lord shows mercy to those who love and obey Him, but He repays the wicked to their face.

> Deut. 7:9 "Therefore know that the Lord your God, He *is* God, the faithful God who keeps covenant and mercy for a thousand generations with those who love Him and keep His commandments;
> Deut. 7:10 And He repays those who hate Him to their face, to destroy them. He will not be slack with him who hates Him; He will repay him to his face.

America doesn't need to simply unite, rebuild, recover, and become stronger as we often hear in the wake of disasters. Christians—you and I—must lead our nation in repentance, or we too will perish.

> Isa. 55:6 Seek the Lord while He may be found, call upon Him while He is near.
> Isa. 55:7 Let the wicked forsake his way, and the unrighteous man his thoughts; let him return to the Lord, and He will have mercy on him; and to our God, for He will abundantly pardon.

May God give us grace to humble ourselves under His mighty hand of discipline while there's still time!

3- Stand In The Gap

I sought for a man among them who would stand in the gap before Me...Eze. 22:30

3-1 While There's Still Time

Christians are the conscience of America, and we are responsible for our nation. God has chosen to work through a faithful remnant.

> Pro. 29:8 Scornful men bring a city into a snare: <u>but wise *men* turn away wrath</u>.

Although we are pilgrims in this world with a heavenly calling, we are still responsible for our influence. When Israel went into captivity, God commanded them through Jeremiah:

> Jer. 29:5 Build houses and dwell *in them;* plant gardens and eat their fruit.
> Jer. 29:6 Take wives and beget sons and daughters;

> and take wives for your sons and give your daughters to husbands, so that they may bear sons and daughters—that you may be increased there, and not diminished.
> Jer. 29:7 And seek the peace of the city <u>where I have caused you to be carried away captive</u>, and <u>pray to the Lord for it; for in its peace you will have peace</u>.

The inhabitants of Sodom would have been spared if the Lord had found ten righteous persons there.

> Gen. 18:32 Then he said, "Let not the Lord be angry, and I will speak but once more: Suppose ten should be found there?" And He said, "<u>I will not destroy *it* for the sake of ten</u>."

We are to be salt and light where God has placed us. We are to pray for our leaders. By God's grace, we are to be the best neighbors, the best citizens, and the best Americans we can be. There is no conflict between Christianity and patriotism, between love of God and love of country. We can render unto Caesar that which is Caesar's and to God that which is God's. We are our brother's keeper, and we will one day give account for our stewardship.

It is time we began to speak up and let our voice be heard. We must raise the alarm and call God's people to pray and seek His face. We must become catalysts for revival in our churches by seeking God and encouraging others to do the same. We must become prayer warriors standing in the gap for our families, our churches, our cities, and our nation.

God has been sending calamities on America—hurricanes, forest fires, earthquakes, terror attacks, mass shootings, economic disasters, chaos in our nation's capital, riots in our streets, and at the time of this writing, a major pandemic that has rocked Wall Street and brought America and the world to a virtual standstill. These are God's wake-up calls for a people who have become deaf and blind to His reproofs.

Be honest, are you *more* obedient because of recent tragedies? Are you *more* faithful in your worship and church attendance? Do you pray, study, give, and witness *more*? I am afraid the truth is our lives have changed very little in response to these calamities even though they have been increasing in frequency and intensity. God has blessed us more than any people, and we have presumed on His goodness, taken advantage of His mercy, and ignored His warnings, not unlike ancient Israel.

> Isa. 9:13 For the people do not turn to Him who strikes them, nor do they seek the Lord of hosts.

Today, the Lord is looking for repentance, confession, and obedience, not from the world but from you and me. He is looking for us to admit we have walked in our pride and presumption, we have refused His correction, and He has brought these evils upon us. God is chastising America, and we must recognize what He is doing and join Him through personal repentance and corporate confession while there's still time. However, if we do not join God *now* in His work of repentance and revival, we will soon witness His work of judgment and destruction. The choice is ours.

3-2 A Chosen Intercessor

Daniel was a captive in the land of the Chaldeans or modern day Iraq. He had been deported from his native Judea along with thousands of others to serve Nebuchadnezzar, King of Babylon. As a youth, Daniel had been selected and educated to be an adviser to his new Sovereign and had continued in that capacity even after the fall of Babylon to the kingdom of the Medes and Persians.

Captivity was an extreme way God corporately disciplined His people. It was not the norm. It was not God's best. It was not God's desire for His people, but it was His will in light of their sin. Since captivity was a corporate measure, the righteous suffered along with the wicked.

Daniel became aware of God's activity as he studied the prophecy of Jeremiah written some 70 years previously.

> Dan. 9:1 In the first year of Darius the son of Ahasuerus, of the lineage of the Medes, who was made king over the realm of the Chaldeans—
> Dan. 9:2 In the first year of his reign I, Daniel, understood by the books the number of the years *specified* by the word of the Lord through Jeremiah the prophet, that He would accomplish seventy years in the desolations of Jerusalem.

Spending time in the word enabled Daniel to recognize God's activity, and it is essential for us if we want to join God in what He is doing today. As Daniel read from a copy of the scroll of Jeremiah brought by the Jews to Babylon, he realized the end of the captivity and the time of their restoration was near.

At this juncture, Daniel distinguished himself as a man of faith by what he did *not* do as well as what he did. He did not say, "God is sovereign; He does whatever He pleases. He doesn't need me." He did not think, "This is all very interesting, but I will just watch to see what happens next." He did not say to himself, "Well, things are not so bad here in Persia. Besides, I hold a very responsible position as the King's servant." And he certainly did not tell God, "If something needs to be done, let somebody else do it."

The awareness that God was about to restore and build Jerusalem dramatically affected Daniel's behavior. He saw it as God's invitation to join Him in what He was doing. In the following verses, we see Daniel's response.

> Dan. 9:3 Then I set my face toward the Lord God to make request by prayer and supplications, with fasting, sackcloth, and ashes.
> Dan. 9:4 And I prayed to the Lord my God, and made confession, and said, "O Lord, great and awesome God, who keeps His covenant and mercy with those who love Him, and with those who keep His commandments,

Most of us want a spiritual breakthrough with little effort on our part; we want the prize without paying the price. As Leonard Ravenhill said, "Alas and alas, this is a rush age. If we could, we would rush God, too. We want big blessings for small installments, the birth of revival but not the pain of birth." The revelation Daniel received from the Word of God caused him to diligently seek the Lord.

Why do you think God chose Daniel as an intercessor? It was not because he had plenty of time or that he was old with nothing better to do. Like David, Daniel was a man after God's heart. God knew He could trust Daniel to give expression to His heart for Israel. He set his face to pray earnestly for his people. To set one's face conveys the idea of steadfast determination.

> Luke 9:51 Now it came to pass, when the time had come for Him to be received up, that <u>He steadfastly set His face to go to Jerusalem,</u>
> Luke 9:52 And sent messengers before His face. And as they went, they entered a village of the Samaritans, to prepare for Him.
> Luke 9:53 But they did not receive Him, because <u>His face was *set* for the journey to Jerusalem</u>.

When it came to seeking the Lord on behalf of his nation, Daniel let nothing distract him. It became his holy preoccupation.

Repentance was the will of God for His people, and Daniel gave expression to God's heart. Today, I believe God is again calling His people to repentance. Will you hear His voice? Can He trust you to give expression to His heart?

Daniel's prayer and supplications were accompanied by fasting, sackcloth, and ashes. Refraining from food, donning rough, uncomfortable clothing, and sprinkling ashes on his head were outward evidences of his inner brokenness and humility. His outward affliction reflected his inward desire and determination to get in touch with God. However, do not misunderstand. God does not hear our prayers *because* we afflict ourselves, but *when* we afflict ourselves. We cannot impress God or earn His favor, but when our outward actions reflect the contrition of our hearts, God is pleased to hear our cries. To the soft, affluent believers in America this may seem strange. However, when we become desperate enough to fast from food, sleep, entertainment, and a host of other things that hinder our seeking the Lord, then we too will have what we ask from God.

3-3 The Principle Of "Standing"

The word *confess* in the New Testament is a compound of two Greek words—homo: "the same" and logeo: "to speak or say." Therefore, the basic meaning is to say the same thing that God is saying or to agree with Him.

> Dan. 9:4 And I prayed to the Lord my God, and made confession, and said, "O Lord, great and awesome God, who keeps His covenant and mercy with those who love Him, and with those who keep His commandments,

Daniel's confession began with an acknowledgment of God's glory followed by an appeal to His covenant relationship with the nation of Israel. Then he accepted his responsibility as being part of the problem as well as the solution.

Daniel was a godly man, walking in obedience to the Lord. Ezekiel names him as one of God's most powerful intercessors.

> Eze. 14:13 "Son of man, when a land sins against Me by persistent unfaithfulness, I will stretch out My hand against it; I will cut off its supply of bread, send famine on it, and cut off man and beast from it.
> Eze. 14:14 Even *if* these three men, Noah, Daniel, and Job, were in it, they would deliver *only* themselves by their righteousness," says the Lord GOD.

Although Daniel was a righteous man, he was also part of a nation that had rebelled against God. The Lord had redeemed

Israel to be His special treasure of all the nations on the earth. At Sinai, He brought them into relationship with Himself through a blood covenant with specific privileges and responsibilities.

> Heb. 9:18 Therefore not even the first *covenant* was dedicated without blood.
> Heb. 9:19 For when Moses had spoken every precept to all the people according to the law, he took the blood of calves and goats, with water, scarlet wool, and hyssop, and sprinkled both the book itself and all the people,
> Heb. 9:20 Saying, "This is the blood of the covenant which God has commanded you.

Daniel had a *personal* relationship with the God of Abraham, but as a member of the community of Israel, he participated in a *corporate* relationship as well. Personally, Daniel may have been blameless, but corporately, he shared in the guilt of the nation because he was an Israelite. The upside of this relationship was that when God blessed the nation, everyone shared the good fortune. The downside was that when God disciplined His people, the righteous suffered along with the wicked.

Daniel's participation in the covenant community of Israel also gave him standing before God to intercede for his people. Simply put, *standing* is a legal term meaning the right or ability to argue a case before a judge. Without it, a judge would dismiss the case because the plaintiff has no legitimate right to argue his case.

For example, in the divine economy, parents are charged with the responsibility to raise their children in the fear and admonition of the Lord. Given their accountability before God, no one can pray with greater authority for their children because no one has their responsibility and as a consequence, their standing.

As a participant in the covenant and a member of the Jewish nation, Daniel had standing—the legal right to plead for Israel before the Judge of all the earth. He could confess his sins, the sins of his leaders, and the sins of his people. He could remind

God of His covenant, and he could plead for mercy on behalf of the entire nation. Daniel made use of his standing by including himself throughout his prayer.

* We have sinned, committed iniquity, done wickedly, and rebelled.

  Dan. 9:5 We have sinned and committed iniquity, we have done wickedly and rebelled, even by departing from Your precepts and Your judgments.
  Dan. 9:6 Neither have we heeded Your servants the prophets, who spoke in Your name to our kings and our princes, to our fathers and all the people of the land.

  Dan. 9:9 To the Lord our God *belong* mercy and forgiveness, though we have rebelled against Him.
  Dan. 9:10 We have not obeyed the voice of the Lord our God, to walk in His laws, which He set before us by His servants the prophets.

* We, our kings, princes, and fathers deserve God's judgment.

  Dan. 9:8 "O Lord, to us *belongs* shame of face, to our kings, our princes, and our fathers, because we have sinned against You.

* God is responsible for this; He has judged us as He promised.

  Dan. 9:11 Yes, all Israel has transgressed Your law, and has departed so as not to obey Your voice; therefore the curse and the oath written in the Law of Moses the servant of God have been poured out on us, because we have sinned against Him.
  Dan. 9:12 And He has confirmed His words, which He spoke against us and against our judges who judged us, by bringing upon us a great disaster; for under the whole heaven such has never been done as what has been done to Jerusalem.

* We have stubbornly resisted God's discipline.

> Dan. 9:13 As *it is* written in the Law of Moses, all this disaster has come upon us; yet we have not made our prayer before the Lord our God, that we might turn from our iniquities and understand Your truth.

In Daniel's confession, he spoke for past generations, for himself and his generation, for their kings, princes, judges, and for the entire nation.

> Dan. 9:7 O Lord, righteousness *belongs* to You, but to us shame of face, as *it is* this day—to the men of Judah, to the inhabitants of Jerusalem and all Israel, those near and those far off in all the countries to which You have driven them, because of the unfaithfulness which they have committed against You.

> Dan. 9:16 "O Lord, according to all Your righteousness, I pray, let Your anger and Your fury be turned away from Your city Jerusalem, Your holy mountain; because for our sins, and for the iniquities of our fathers, Jerusalem and Your people *are* a reproach to all *those* around us.

God has not made a covenant with America as He did with Israel, and we are not His chosen people. However, as citizens you and I have standing to plead for our nation. We can stand in the gap and make a wall on behalf of America that God should not destroy it. Moreover, as those who have been redeemed by the blood of Jesus and enjoy the privileges and responsibilities of the New Covenant, we have access to the throne of God and standing to argue our case before the Judge of all the Earth.

Nevertheless, to exercise our standing and intercede with authority for America, we must agree with God. We must be identified with His purposes, and we must say the same thing He is saying. As our oneness with God deepens, the efficacy of our intercession will also increase.

3-4 Corporate Confession

God relates to groups as well as to individuals. Most believers understand personal confession of sin. However, fewer understand or exercise their corporate responsibilities as when God deals with families, churches, and nations.

That God deals with corporate bodies is clearly seen in the messages to the seven churches of Asia Minor. For example, John wrote these words to the church at Ephesus.

> Rev. 2:4 Nevertheless I have *this* against you, that you have left your first love.
> Rev. 2:5 Remember therefore from where you have fallen; repent and do the first works, or else I will come to you quickly and remove your lampstand from its place—unless you repent.

The message was written to "the angel of the church at Ephesus," but the letter was for the believers who made up the church. The threatened discipline was for the group because the sin was corporate. When corporate entities sin against God, corporate repentance and confession is necessary.

As a member of the community of Israel, Daniel suffered personally when God chastised the nation just as Christians in America suffer when disasters strike. However, Daniel's identity as a Jew also gave him standing to confess the corporate sins of his people and plead for God's corporate forgiveness.

> Dan. 9:16 "O Lord, according to all Your righteousness, I pray, let Your anger and Your fury be turned away from Your city Jerusalem, Your holy mountain; because for our sins, and for the iniquities of our fathers, Jerusalem and Your people *are* a reproach to all *those* around us.
> Dan. 9:17 Now therefore, our God, hear the prayer of Your servant, and his supplications, and for the Lord's sake cause Your face to shine on Your sanctuary, which is desolate.

> Dan. 9:18 O my God, incline Your ear and hear; open Your eyes and see our desolations, and the city which is called by Your name; for we do not present our supplications before You because of our righteous deeds, but because of Your great mercies.
> Dan. 9:19 O Lord, hear! O Lord, forgive! O Lord, listen and act! Do not delay for Your own sake, my God, for Your city and Your people are called by Your name."

The implications of this principle are timely and significant. As Americans, you and I can do as Daniel did for his people. We have standing to speak to God on behalf of our nation. Like Daniel, we can acknowledge our corporate sin and disobedience. On behalf of our leaders past and present, we can confess our national sins and acknowledge God's righteous judgment. We can admit that God has afflicted us because we have stubbornly resisted His discipline. Moreover, as believers we have an additional blessing—direct access to the throne of God to plead for His mercy and forgiveness for America. What an awesome privilege and responsibility we have for such a time as this!

Finally, notice that throughout his confession, Daniel was very careful to justify God. He called attention to God's faithfulness, mercy, and righteousness, but never once faulted God for Israel's plight.

> Dan. 9:7 O Lord, righteousness *belongs* to You, but to us shame of face...

> Dan. 9:14 Therefore the Lord has kept the disaster in mind, and brought it upon us; for the Lord our God *is* righteous in all the works which He does, though we have not obeyed His voice.

Confession includes agreeing with God not only about what we have done but what He has done. To fail to agree with God is to deny the truth and call God a liar.

> 1 John 1:10 If we say that we have not sinned, we make Him a liar, and His word is not in us.

As Americans, we must admit that we have deeply offended God. We must also admit that He has brought a great evil upon us. This is the essence of confession.

> Lev. 26:40 But if they confess their iniquity and the iniquity of their fathers, with their unfaithfulness in which they were unfaithful to me,
> Lev. 26:41 And that I also have walked contrary to them and have brought them into the land of their enemies; if their uncircumcised hearts are humbled, and they accept of their guilt:

Acknowledging that we have walked contrary to God by breaking His holy law *and* that He has walked contrary to us by bringing evil upon us are the two things that we resist at all cost. Admitting that we are wrong *and* that God is sovereign strike at the very heart of our fallen human nature.

When Satan tempted our parents he offered them a life of freedom and independence without accountability. However, contrary to prevailing sentiment, we are not free to do as we please or free from the consequences of our choices. By acknowledging our sin and God's discipline, we repudiate both lies.

3-5 Arguing With God

The first time I heard this expression I immediately reacted, thinking, "Who am I to disagree with the Almighty, All-knowing, All-present, Eternal God?" Of course, I did not understand the concept nor had I been shown Biblical examples of this powerful and prevalent practice. However, the more I studied the prayers of Scripture, the more I realized that arguing with God was not trying to convince Him to change His mind, but allowing Him to change my mind and build my faith by bringing me into oneness and agreement with Himself.

Indeed, arguing with God is just the opposite of disagreement. It is actually demonstrating your agreement with God by giving

Him reasons to grant your requests based upon what He has revealed about Himself (His promises, attributes, will, ways, purposes, etc.).

Moses appealed to the Lord's reputation, oath, and covenant promises to Israel as reasons why He should not destroy them for worshipping the golden calf.

> Ex. 32:12 Why should the Egyptians speak, and say, 'He brought them out to harm them, to kill them in the mountains, and to consume them from the face of the earth'? Turn from Your fierce wrath, and relent from this harm to Your people.
> Ex. 32:13 Remember Abraham, Isaac, and Israel, Your servants, to whom You swore by Your own self, and said to them, 'I will multiply your descendants as the stars of heaven; and all this land that I have spoken of I give to your descendants, and they shall inherit *it* forever.'"

As Jesus faced the suffering of the cross, He also gave the Father a reason for hearing His prayer.

> John 17:1 Jesus spoke these words, lifted up His eyes to heaven, and said: "Father, the hour has come. Glorify Your Son, that Your Son also may glorify You,

Like a lawyer in a courtroom, Daniel presented his case before the Lord. He reminded himself as he reminded God of the following evidence in consideration.

* He called the Lord's attention to His covenant relationship with Israel.

> Dan. 9:4 And I prayed to the Lord my God, and made confession, and said, "O Lord, great and awesome God, who keeps His covenant and mercy with those who love Him, and with those who keep His commandments,

* He reminded God's of His righteous character.

> Dan. 9:7 O Lord, righteousness *belongs* to You, but to us shame of face, as *it is* this day—to the men of Judah, to the inhabitants of Jerusalem and all Israel, those near and those far off in all the countries to which You have driven them, because of the unfaithfulness which they have committed against You.

> Dan. 9:14 Therefore the Lord has kept the disaster in mind, and brought it upon us; for the Lord our God *is* righteous in all the works which He does, though we have not obeyed His voice.

* He appealed to God's great faithfulness, mercy, and forgiveness.

> Dan. 9:4 And I prayed to the Lord my God, and made confession, and said, "O Lord, great and awesome God, who keeps His covenant and mercy with those who love Him, and with those who keep His commandments,

> Dan. 9:9 To the Lord our God *belong* mercy and forgiveness, though we have rebelled against Him.

> Dan. 9:18 O my God, incline Your ear and hear; open Your eyes and see our desolations, and the city which is called by Your name; for we do not present our supplications before You because of our righteous deeds, but because of Your great mercies.

* He reminded God that His honor and reputation were on the line.

> Dan. 9:15 And now, O Lord our God, who brought Your people out of the land of Egypt with a mighty hand, and made Yourself a name, as *it is* this day—we have sinned, we have done wickedly!

> Dan. 9:17 Now therefore, our God, hear the prayer of Your servant, and his supplications, and for the

> Lord's sake cause Your face to shine on Your sanctuary, which is desolate.
> Dan. 9:18 O my God, incline Your ear and hear; open Your eyes and see our desolations, and the city which is called by Your name; for we do not present our supplications before You because of our righteous deeds, but because of Your great mercies.
> Dan. 9:19 O Lord, hear! O Lord, forgive! O Lord, listen and act! Do not delay for Your own sake, my God, for Your city and Your people are called by Your name."

Daniel knew that what happened to Israel was a reflection on their God because they were called by His name. By basing his prayer on God's covenant, character, will, and reputation, Daniel demonstrated to himself that the Lord had something to lose by rejecting his petition and something to gain by granting it. As he worked through this process, Daniel did not convince the Lord to change His mind, but he allowed God to adjust his thinking, build his faith, and bring him into deeper oneness with Himself *which is a key to prevailing prayer*.

How does this apply to us as we intercede for America? Ask yourself a question: Why should God spare us? The abortion holocaust alone is reason enough for God to destroy this nation. God judged Israel for sacrificing their children on the altars of Molech, and He will not let us go unpunished.

> Ps. 106:37 They even sacrificed their sons and their daughters to demons,
> Ps. 106:38 And shed innocent blood, the blood of their sons and daughters, whom they sacrificed to the idols of Canaan; and the land was polluted with blood.
> Ps. 106:39 Thus they were defiled by their own works, and played the harlot by their own deeds.
> Ps. 106:40 Therefore the wrath of the Lord was kindled against His people, so that He abhorred His own inheritance.

Since the Supreme Court decision legalizing abortion in 1973, we have brutally murdered more than 61,000,000 of our children, and their blood daily cries to God for justice. Our nation stands guilty and condemned. How shall we escape? What can we say in our defense? We have no righteousness to plead, but there is hope.

Daniel's appeal was to God's great mercies rather than to their righteous deeds.

> Dan. 9:18 O my God, incline Your ear and hear; open Your eyes and see our desolations, and the city which is called by Your name; for we do not present our supplications before You because of our righteous deeds, but because of Your great mercies.

If God hears our prayer and restrains His wrath against America, it will not be because of our righteousness either. The basis for our appeal must also be the Lord's great mercy. If we received what we deserved, we would have no hope. However, God is abundant in mercy.

> Ps. 86:5 For You, Lord, *are* good, and ready to forgive, and abundant in mercy to all those who call upon You.

Do you know what matters to God? Do you desire His will above all else? Are you identified with His purposes? Do you know how to make an appeal? When you pray, do you give God a reason for granting your petition?

3-6 Rx For Revival

As Daniel interceded for his people, it is important to recognize that he met the conditions God established for spiritual renewal and restoration to the land. In the Law of Moses, God prescribed Israel's discipline and the precise steps required for the nation to return to Him. The Lord promised they would suffer as captives in their enemies' lands on account of their iniquities and the iniquities of their fathers.

> Lev. 26:39 And those of you who are left shall waste away in their iniquity in your enemies' lands; also in their fathers' iniquities, which are with them, they shall waste away.

Their confession of repentance had to include the admission of their wrongdoing and the wrong done by their fathers *and* the acknowledgement that God had judged them for their sin by bringing them into subjection to their enemies.

> Lev. 26:40 *But* if they confess their iniquity and the iniquity of their fathers, with their unfaithfulness in which they were unfaithful to Me, and that they also have walked contrary to Me,
> Lev. 26:41 And *that* I also have walked contrary to them and have brought them into the land of their enemies; if their uncircumcised hearts are humbled, and they accept their guilt—

Humbling their proud hearts and accepting their guilt required both of the following components:

- They had to see their suffering as the result of their sin and the sins of previous generations.
- They had to acknowledge that their present distress was the direct result of God's judgment, not random chance.

God's hand of judgment lies heavy on America, but not for the reason most Christians believe. It is easy for us to blame the wicked for the troubles we face as a nation, but the responsibility lies much closer to home. Wickedness abounds when there is no godly influence in society.

> Ps. 12:1 Help, Lord, for the godly man ceases! For the faithful disappear from among the sons of men.

When the church fails to be the church—when the salt has lost its saltiness, when the lamp is no longer giving light to all who are in the house, when you can't tell Christians from the world—evil goes unchecked and judgment ultimately falls.

What the church needs today is not, as is often suggested, merely cosmetic changes—new ideas, new methods, new programs, new music, more casual dress, screens, projectors, drama, shorter more positive sermons, etc. God is not looking for superficial changes that fail to address the real problem of sin. He is searching for men and women across America who will make up the hedge and stand in the gap before Him on behalf of this nation that He should not destroy it. That means confessing sin and pleading for forgiveness. It means becoming a holy people for a holy God.

You may not feel you are personally responsible for what has happened to our country, but you are a citizen and you have standing. When God judges, we will suffer along with the wicked, or we can do what Daniel did and begin to pour out our hearts to the Lord.

Confession of sin and acknowledgement of God's discipline are essential for revival and awakening. Each time we face a major calamity, politicians always respond the same way. In pride, they refuse to acknowledge God's displeasure, and they assure us we will come back stronger than ever. To admit wrongdoing is viewed as weakness and to acknowledge divine judgment is not politically correct. However, without repentance—a radical change in our thinking—God's chastisement will only become more severe. Our leaders may never do this, but we can do it for them.

God holds out a powerful promise of hope to us in the book of Jeremiah.

> Jer. 18:7 The instant I speak concerning a nation and concerning a kingdom, to pluck up, to pull down, and to destroy *it,*
> Jer. 18:8 If that nation against whom I have spoken turns from its evil, I will relent of the disaster that I thought to bring upon it.

In the book of Jonah, the Lord spoke through His prophet concerning the destruction of Nineveh.

> Jonah 3:4 And Jonah began to enter the city on the first day's walk. Then he cried out and said, "Yet forty days, and Nineveh shall be overthrown!"

The people believed God and repented from "the least to the greatest." Even the King removed his royal robes, and put on sackcloth and ashes. He called the people to prayer and fasting, and God heard their cry.

> Jonah 3:10 Then God saw their works, that they turned from their evil way; and God relented from the disaster that He had said He would bring upon them, and He did not do it.

God has fashioned a disaster and devised a plan against America as He did against ancient Israel. The evidence of His displeasure is unmistakable, and the solution to the problem remains the same.

> Jer. 18:11 Now therefore, speak to the men of Judah and to the inhabitants of Jerusalem, saying, 'Thus says the Lord: "Behold, I am fashioning a disaster and devising a plan against you. Return now every one from his evil way, and make your ways and your doings good."

Will you agree with God about America? Will you say what He is saying? Will you tell Him…

- We have sinned, committed iniquity, and rebelled.

- We have stubbornly resisted Your discipline.

- We have walked contrary to You, and You have walked contrary to us.

Will you speak for America?

- Will you speak for yourself, your generation, and past generations?

- Will you speak on behalf of our fathers, our leaders, and our judges?

This is what it means to make up the hedge, to stand in the gap.

Revival is possible, but it must begin with those who understand what is happening and know what to do. The great English preacher, Charles Spurgeon said, “Whenever God determines to do a great work, He first sets His people to pray.” Do you hear His call? While there’s still time, will you become an intercessor for America?

4- Warfare Praying

For we do not wrestle against flesh and blood...Eph. 6:12

4-1 Imprecatory Psalms

At one time or another, most of us have found comfort and encouragement by reading the psalms of David. One reason we love and identify with the songs of "the sweet singer of Israel" is because they speak to our deepest needs and give expression to our hearts' desires. However, there is a genre of psalms that many believers do not know how to understand and utilize. They are not psalms of praise, blessing, confession, thanksgiving, or petition. They are called imprecatory (im'-pre-ca-tory) psalms, and they seem strange because of their content and seeming harshness.

Some commentators are dismissive of them as sub-Christian and ethically inferior to the higher teachings of the New Testament. Nevertheless, they were included in the sacred canon of Scripture and must therefore be inspired and applicable to life. Jesus did not differentiate between noble psalms and defective psalms. When He appeared to His disciples following His resurrection, He reminded them of the prophecies concerning Himself written in the Law, the Prophets, and *the Psalms*.

> Luke 24:44 Then He said to them, "These *are* the words which I spoke to you while I was still with you, that all things must be fulfilled which were written in the Law of Moses and *the* Prophets and *the* Psalms concerning Me."

The New Testament writers, the early church, and subsequent generations of believers have continued to reverence, teach, and love the Psalms as they do all of the Bible.

> 2 Tim. 3:16 All Scripture *is* given by inspiration of God, and *is* profitable for doctrine, for reproof, for correction, for instruction in righteousness,
> 2 Tim. 3:17 That the man of God may be complete, thoroughly equipped for every good work.

Yet, the *imprecatory psalms* still do not seem to be as much appreciated or utilized as other genres. This has been true in the American church because of the predominance of the Christian faith and the resultant freedom we have enjoyed in this country. Throughout our history, the vast majority of American believers have not been marginalized or persecuted. Consequently, we have had little occasion to appreciate psalms that call on God to vindicate us and judge our enemies.

> Ps. 5:10 Pronounce them guilty, O God! Let them fall by their own counsels; cast them out in the multitude of their transgressions, for they have rebelled against You.

> Ps. 79:6 Pour out Your wrath on the nations that do not know You, and on the kingdoms that do not call on Your name.
> Ps. 79:7 For they have devoured Jacob, and laid waste his dwelling place.

However, times are quickly changing. As more and more Christians find themselves the targets of false accusation and persecution, I believe the *imprecatory psalms* will become more relevant and important in our public and private worship.

Psalm 83 is a prayer of Asaph, not of David. Commentators disagree as to the occasion of its composition. Some think it refers to a war with Syria in the time of David, while others assign it to the reign of Jehoshaphat. It may be that it relates to a threatened invasion in the past, or it could be prophetic of a future attempt to annihilate Israel. In any case, there is an amazing parallel between the description of Israel in relation to her enemies and the struggle of conservative America against the forces of secular humanism threatening the foundations on which our nation was established. By comparing the two struggles, we will see a very relevant application of imprecatory psalms and learn how "to make a wall, and stand in the gap" for America.

4-2 Boldness In Prayer

One of the notable things about this prayer was the boldness of Asaph. He began his supplications with a rather shocking declaration.

> Ps. 83:1 Do not keep silent, O God! Do not hold Your peace, and do not be still, O God!

Imagine telling the omnipotent, righteous Judge of all the earth, "Speak up! Do not remain silent any longer! Get busy and help us!" To the uninitiated, it might seem that Asaph is being presumptuous and irreverent, or that he is trying to provoke God to do something He really doesn't want to do. Actually, his boldness is based on his understanding of God's covenant, God's promises, and God's will for Israel as well as the activity and objectives of Israel's enemies. Similarly, we may be bold in our praying when we understand the will of God and His promises to us, His children.

After being released by the authorities following the healing of the lame man at the Beautiful Gate, Peter and John returned to the other disciples and held a prayer meeting. Notice the boldness of the united prayer of those early believers.

> Acts 4:24 So when they heard that, they raised their voice to God with one accord and said: "Lord, You *are* God, who made heaven and earth and the sea, and all that is in them,
> Acts 4:25 Who by the mouth of Your servant David have said: 'Why did the nations rage, and the people plot vain things?
> Acts 4:26 The kings of the earth took their stand, and the rulers were gathered together against the Lord and against His Christ.'
> Acts 4: 27 "For truly against Your holy Servant Jesus, whom You anointed, both Herod and Pontius Pilate, with the Gentiles and the people of Israel, were gathered together
> Acts 4:28 To do whatever Your hand and Your purpose determined before to be done.
> Acts 4:29 Now, Lord, look on their threats, and grant to Your servants that with all boldness they may speak Your word,
> Acts 4:30 By stretching out Your hand to heal, and that signs and wonders may be done through the name of Your holy Servant Jesus."

The early church was bold in prayer because they understood what was happening from Psalm 2 which they quoted in their supplication. They also knew what Jesus had promised.

> John 14:12 "Most assuredly, I say to you, he who believes in Me, the works that I do he will do also; and greater *works* than these he will do, because I go to My Father.
> John 14:13 And whatever you ask in My name, that I will do, that the Father may be glorified in the Son.
> John 14:14 If you ask anything in My name, I will do *it*.

> John 15:7 If you abide in Me, and My words abide in you, you will ask what you desire, and it shall be done for you.

Furthermore, they understood what Jesus had commanded them to do.

> Acts 1:8 But you shall receive power when the Holy Spirit has come upon you; and you shall be witnesses to Me in Jerusalem, and in all Judea and Samaria, and to the end of the earth."

The early church discerned what was happening from God's word, believed in Jesus, and did what He said. That is how we can be bold in our prayers as well.

4-3 Presenting The Case

In verses 2-5, Asaph described what was happening as he carefully laid out his case before the LORD.

> Ps. 83:2 For behold, Your enemies make a tumult; and those who hate You have lifted up their head.
> Ps. 83:3 They have taken crafty counsel against Your people, and consulted together against Your sheltered ones.
> Ps. 83:4 They have said, "Come, and let us cut them off from *being* a nation, that the name of Israel may be remembered no more."
> Ps. 83:5 For they have consulted together with one consent; they form a confederacy against You:

Asaph explained what their enemies were doing but not so much in terms of how it affected his people but how it affected God. He pointed out that they were enemies of the Lord.

- Your enemies make a tumult;

- Those who hate You have lifted up their head.

- They have taken crafty counsel against Your people, and consulted together against Your sheltered ones.

- They form a confederacy against You:

Asaph also demonstrated that the goals of the enemy alliance were contrary to the will, word, and purpose of God.

- They have said, "Come, and let us cut them off from *being* a nation, that the name of Israel may be remembered no more."

When Israel sinned regarding the golden calf, God was angry and threatened their destruction. Moses took this same approach in his intercession. He argued that to destroy the people was contrary to the Lord's purpose in delivering them from bondage, His oath that He had sworn to their fathers, and His promise to give them the land of Canaan. Obviously, God understood the contradiction, but He was teaching Moses what it meant to be an intercessor. Moses needed to learn how to merge in his heart the purposes of God and the welfare of His people without denying either. Job described this function of an intercessor in response to his friends.

> Job 9:32 "For He is not a man, as I am, that I may answer Him, and that we should go to court together.
> Job 9:33 Nor is there any mediator (intercessor) between us, who may lay his hand on us both.

What reasons can you marshal for God to send revival and awakening to America? How would God's agenda be furthered by sparing us? Can you identify some arguments that would encourage you to believe the Lord will hear your prayers for spiritual renewal in America.

4-4 Discerning The Enemies' Strategy

Looking at verses 2-5, it doesn't seem that much has changed over the millennia. In fact, we see many of the same tactics being used today by the champions of secular humanism as they conspire, unite, vilify, threaten, and assail those who fear God.

> Ps. 83:2 For behold, Your enemies make a tumult; and those who hate You have lifted up their head.
> Ps. 83:3 They have taken crafty counsel against Your people, and consulted together against Your sheltered ones.
> Ps. 83:4 They have said, "Come, and let us cut them off from *being* a nation, that the name of Israel may be remembered no more."
> Ps. 83:5 For they have consulted together with one consent; they form a confederacy against You:

In light of these verses, consider some of the strategies Satan has been using against God-fearing Americans and conservative Christians? Daily the enemy uses liberal educators to indoctrinate the next generation and disparage the Biblical record through pseudo-science, false-philosophies, intimidation, and humiliation. The entertainment industry pours out a steady stream of TV shows, movies, internet games, music videos, and pornography that desensitizes the public through exposure to evil and aids the liberal agenda. Activist judges, legislating from the bench, advance a godless moral and social program that would never be approved at the ballot box. Liberal politicians and business leaders leverage social, economic, and legal pressure to force conformity to their morality and belief system.

Never before have so many institutions of American life been so focused in their efforts to undermine the values and principles that have made our nation great. Their attacks against Biblical morality, marriage and family life as God ordained it, character-centered education, a Christian work ethic, religious liberty, the sanctity of life, fiscal responsibility, freedom of conscience, the rule of law, and equality for all are unrelenting.

Paul wrote to the Corinthians reminding them of the devil's schemes and warning them of the consequences of being ignorant of his tactics.

> 2 Cor. 2:11 Lest Satan should take advantage of us; for we are not ignorant of his devices.

The enemy has many weapons that he employs against God's people. Are you ignorant of his devices? Do you recognize Satan's attacks? To be effective intercessors for America, we must discern his strategies and be alert to his activity.

4-5 Identifying God's Enemies

In his prayer, Asaph named names. He called out those who were the enemies of Israel, but more importantly he identified those who were the enemies of God.

> Ps. 83:6 The tabernacles of Edom, and the Ishmaelites; of Moab, and the Hagarenes;
> Ps. 83:7 Gebal, and Ammon, and Amalek; the Philistines with the inhabitants of Tyre;
> Ps. 83:8 Assur also is joined with them: they have helped the children of Lot. *Selah*

Historically, these nations had resisted and warred against the Jews and thus opposed the purposes of God. Edom was the kingdom established by Esau's descendants. They were joined by the descendants of Ishmael also known as Medianites. Moab and Ammon were Lot's two sons and became nations in their own right. The Hagarenes are doubtless the descendants of Hagar, the maid Sarah gave to Abraham to obtain children by her. Gebal is thought to be one of the clans of Edom living near the Dead Sea. The Amalekites inhabited parts of Canaan and opposed Israel's conquest of the land. The Philistines or Palestinians were also some of the original inhabitants of Canaan whom the Lord commanded Israel to dispossess. The inhabitants of Tyre identified an ancient Phoenician city-state on the Mediterranean coast to Israel's north. Northeast of Israel was the powerful kingdom of Assur (Assyria) that was allied with the children of Lot—the kingdoms of Moab and Ammon. These nations with numerically superior armies were strategically located to Judah's north, east, and south. With their backs to the Mediterranean Sea and hemmed in on every remaining side, the Jews seemed to have no hope.

Looking at American life today, it is not difficult to identify the enemies of faith and morality. Ask yourself, "Who are the outspoken enemies of our Christian heritage?" A complete list would be burdensome, but here are some well-known organizations and entities that openly oppose conservative Christian values.

Politics- the Democrat Party, MoveOn, ANTIFA.

Education- National Education Association (NEA).

Civil Rights- American Civil Liberties Union (ACLU), People For The American Way (PFTAW), Planned Parenthood, Southern Poverty And Law Center (SPLC), National Abortion and Reproductive Rights League (NARAL), National Organization For Women (NOW), National Gay and Lesbian Task Force (NGLTF), American Association Of Retired Persons (AARP).

Media- CNN, MSNBC, ABC, CBS, NBC, New York Times.

Entertainment- Disney, Netflix.

Business- Amazon, Apple, IBM, Intel, Verizon. Microsoft, Facebook, Target, Charles Schwab, Home Depot, Macy's,

Religion- National Council of Churches (NCC), and World Council of Churches (WCC).

Environment- Sierra Club, Greenpeace.

Although they purport to stand for the disenfranchised, represent family values, and advocate for good causes, a closer examination reveals otherwise. These organizations and many of the people in them, although blinded by Satan, are the enemies of Christ just as we were at one time.

> Rom. 5:10 For if when we were enemies we were reconciled to God through the death of His Son, much more, having been reconciled, we shall be saved by His life.

Moreover, these organizations represent a powerful alliance of liberal causes that touches on almost every area of American life. With such a broad base of influence, secular progressives also feel confident of victory. To prevail in this spiritual war for the soul of America we must know our enemy and learn to use our weapons.

4-6 Praying God's Will

In his intercession, Asaph appealed to God to judge His enemies as He had done in former times.

> Ps. 83:9 Deal with them as *with* Midian, as *with* Sisera, as *with* Jabin at the Brook Kishon,
> Ps. 83:10 Who perished at En Dor, w*ho* became *as* refuse on the earth.
> Ps. 83:11 Make their nobles like Oreb and like Zeeb, yes, all their princes like Zebah and Zalmunna,

In the days of the Judges, Barak and Deborah had mustered the armies of Israel and led them to defeat Sisera and the armies of Jabin, King of Canaan.

> Judges 4:14 Then Deborah said to Barak, "Up! For this *is* the day in which the Lord has delivered Sisera into your hand. Has not the Lord gone out before you?" So Barak went down from Mount Tabor with ten thousand men following him.
> Judges 4:15 And the Lord routed Sisera and all *his* chariots and all *his* army with the edge of the sword before Barak; and Sisera alighted from *his* chariot and fled away on foot.
> Judges 4:16 But Barak pursued the chariots and the army as far as Harosheth Hagoyim, and all the army of Sisera fell by the edge of the sword; not a man was left.

Gideon and his band of three hundred delivered Israel from a Midianite invasion led by two princes, Oreb and Zeeb, and two kings, Zebah and Zalmunna.

> Judges 7:25 And they took two princes of the Midianites, Oreb and Zeeb; and they slew Oreb upon the rock Oreb, and Zeeb they slew at the winepress of Zeeb, and pursued Midian, and brought the heads of Oreb and Zeeb to Gideon on the other side Jordan.

> Judges 8:21 Then Zebah and Zalmunna said, Rise thou, and fall upon us: for as the man *is, so is* his strength. And Gideon arose, and slew Zebah and Zalmunna, and took away the ornaments that *were* on their camels' necks.

The defeat of Israel's enemies was the will of God, and He accomplished it through the judges He raised up for their deliverance. Similarly, God has raised up Christian leaders all across America who have been sounding the alarm and leading His church to stand against those who would silence our witness to Jesus.

Have you missed the "culture war" that has been raging against the church for years? In an essay entitled *A Religion For A New Age,* atheist John Dunphy described the pivotal yet little recognized role liberal educators have played in the battle for the soul of America.

> "I am convinced that the battle for humankind's future must be waged and won in the public school classroom by teachers who correctly perceive their role as the proselytizers of a new faith: a religion of humanity that recognizes and respects the spark of what theologians call divinity in every human being. These teachers must embody the same selfless dedication as the most rabid fundamentalist preachers, for they will be ministers of another sort, utilizing a classroom instead of a pulpit to convey humanists values in whatever subject they teach, regardless of

> the educational level—preschool day care or large state university. The classroom must and will become an arena of conflict between the old and the new—the rotting corpse of Christianity, together with all its adjacent evils and misery, and the new faith of humanism, resplendent in its promise of a world in which the never-realized Christian ideal of "love thy neighbor" will finally be achieved." (The Humanist, Jan-Feb. 1983, Volume 43, Number 1)

Harvard Professor of Education and Psychiatry, Chester M. Pierce, clearly drew the battle lines in an address to the Association for Childhood Education International in April of 1972 in Denver, Colorado.

> "Every child in America entering school at the age of five is mentally ill because he comes to school with certain allegiances to our Founding Fathers, toward our elected officials, toward his parents, toward a belief in a supernatural being, and toward the sovereignty of this nation as a separate entity. It's up to you as teachers to make all these sick children well—by creating the international child of the future."

What is God's will regarding those who openly oppose the godly values and principles that have helped to foster America's greatness? Is it for Christians to stand aside while they destroy the foundations of our society? I believe it is the will of God for Christians to be salt and light wherever God has placed us, and I believe we have a weapon that will change the course of America if we will use it. F. J. Heugel wrote, "In this atomic age when forces are being released that stagger the thought and imagination of man, it is well to remember that prayer transcends all other forces." Prayer engages the power of God, and with Him nothing is impossible.

Consider how the psalmist's petitions reflect the will and ways of God. Can the imprecatory cries of David, a man after God's own heart, inform our praying for America?

> Ps. 140:4 Keep me, O LORD, from the hands of the wicked; preserve me from the violent man; who have purposed to overthrow my goings.

> Ps. 140:8 Grant not, O LORD, the desires of the wicked: further not his wicked device; *lest* they exalt themselves.
> Ps. 140:9 *As for* the head of those that compass me about, let the mischief of their own lips cover them.

> Ps. 140:11 Let not an evil speaker be established in the earth: evil shall hunt the violent man to overthrow *him*.

4-7 Discerning The Enemies' Objective.

The alliance of nations surrounding Israel described in Psalm 83 wanted what belonged to God. Not unlike the current situation in the Middle East, Israel's neighbors wanted to possess what He had given to His people.

> Ps. 83:12 Who said, Let us take to ourselves the habitations of God in possession.

It has been Satan's goal from the beginning to possess what belongs to God. He was cast out of heaven because he wanted to be like the Most High—to share His glory, position, and rule.

> Isa. 14:13 For you have said in your heart: 'I will ascend into heaven, I will exalt my throne above the stars of God; I will also sit on the mount of the congregation on the farthest sides of the north;
> Isa. 14:14 I will ascend above the heights of the clouds, I will be like the Most High.'

Satan tempted Adam and Eve to sin that he might gain authority over God's creation, and he now rules as "the god of this age" over the race of men.

> Eph. 2:1 And you *He made alive,* who were dead in trespasses and sins,
> Eph. 2:2 In which you once walked according to the course of this world, according to the prince of the power of the air, the spirit who now works in the sons of disobedience,

God chose Jerusalem as the place where He would put His name and receive the worship of His people. Satan exercised control of the city until David captured it from the Jebusites and made it his capital. His son, Solomon, built the house of the Lord, and Jerusalem was the center of Israel's worship during his reign. However, at Solomon's death the kingdom was divided into Northern Israel and Southern Judah with capitals in Samaria and Jerusalem respectively. Satan stole the worship of God when Jeroboam, Israel's first king, set up an idolatrous worship center in Samaria to entice the ten northern tribes away from the temple in Jerusalem. Subsequently, Satan was so successful in infiltrating and corrupting the southern kingdom that in the days of Ezekiel, Jerusalem, the land, the prophets, the priests, the princes and the people were all profane (Eze. 22:1-29). Consequently, the Lord God sent Judah into captivity to Babylon for seventy years.

Following their restoration to the land under Ezra and Nehemiah in the 539 BC, Jerusalem and the temple were rebuilt but never attained to their original glory.

The Babylonian captivity purged the nation of their pagan idolatries, but four hundred years before Christ, Malachi, a post-exilic prophet, described the worship of the LORD in terms of empty religious culture, barren of true heart devotion. By the time of Christ, Satan had consolidated his control and blinded the nation to God's activity.

> Luke 13:34 "O Jerusalem, Jerusalem, the one who kills the prophets and stones those who are sent to her! How often I wanted to gather your children together, as a hen *gathers* her brood under *her* wings, but you were not willing!

> Luke 19:41 Now as He drew near, He saw the city and wept over it,
> Luke 19:42 Saying, "If you had known, even you, especially in this your day, the things *that make* for your peace! But now they are hidden from your eyes.
> Luke 19:43 For days will come upon you when your enemies will build an embankment around you, surround you and close you in on every side,
> Luke 19:44 And level you, and your children within you, to the ground; and they will not leave in you one stone upon another, because you did not know the time of your visitation."

In the present age, the Church is the temple of the Holy Spirit and the dwelling place of God on earth.

> 1 Cor. 3:16 Do you not know that you are the temple of God and *that* the Spirit of God dwells in you?
> 1 Cor. 3:17 If anyone defiles the temple of God, God will destroy him. For the temple of God is holy, which *temple* you are.

Consequently, Satan desires to infiltrate, subvert, and steal God's worship. In the letters to the seven churches of Asia, both Pergamos and Thyatira received similar troubling rebukes.

> Rev. 2:14 But I have a few things against you, because you have there those who hold the doctrine of Balaam, who taught Balak to put a stumbling block before the children of Israel, to eat things sacrificed to idols, and to commit sexual immorality.

> Rev. 2:20 Nevertheless I have a few things against you, because you allow that woman Jezebel, who calls herself a prophetess, to teach and seduce My servants to commit sexual immorality and eat things sacrificed to idols.

In the final days of this age, the man of sin, Satan incarnate, will occupy the Jewish Temple and seek to steal God's worship during the tribulation.

> 2 Thess. 2:3 Let no one deceive you by any means; for *that Day will not come* unless the falling away comes first, and the man of sin is revealed, the son of perdition,
> 2 Thess. 2:4 Who opposes and exalts himself above all that is called God or that is worshiped, so that he sits as God in the temple of God, showing himself that he is God.

At the close of the millennial reign of Jesus Christ, Satan will make his final, unsuccessful bid to possess the habitations of God.

> Rev. 20:7 Now when the thousand years have expired, Satan will be released from his prison
> Rev. 20:8 And will go out to deceive the nations which are in the four corners of the earth, Gog and Magog, to gather them together to battle, whose number *is* as the sand of the sea.
> Rev. 20:9 They went up on the breadth of the earth and surrounded the camp of the saints and the beloved city. And fire came down from God out of heaven and devoured them.

From the beginning, Satan's objective has been to arrogate the worship of the true God to himself and eliminate all who will not submit. He wants for himself all that rightfully belongs to the Creator.

There are those in America today who desire to usurp the place of God. They believe they are the final authority. They want you to believe whatever they say, and they think they know what is best for you and your children. They believe they have the right to decide what is right and wrong. They want to control you, they want to control the media, and they want to decide who will live and who will die. Thankfully, Bible believing Christians and God fearing Americans stand in the way of their utopian dreams. That is why they hate God and hate us.

To be effective in our intercession we must understand the enemy's ultimate objective. Can you recognize where Satan is usurping God's place in your life, family, church, community, and nation? Are you standing against the enemy or silent in the face of his steady advance?

4-8 Prayer In Harmony With God's Word and Ways

Hear the psalmist's plea as he enlists God's help in the battle.

> Ps. 83:13 O my God, make them like the whirling dust, like the chaff before the wind!
> Ps. 83:14 As the fire burns the woods, and as the flame sets the mountains on fire,
> Ps. 83:15 So pursue them with Your tempest, and frighten them with Your storm.
> Ps. 83:16 Fill their faces with shame, that they may seek Your name, O Lord.
> Ps. 83:17 Let them be confounded and dismayed forever; yes, let them be put to shame and perish,

At first glance, it might seem that Asaph was full of spite and personal indignation, like the disciples when they were rebuffed by the Samaritans.

> Luke 9:53 But they did not receive Him, because His face was *set* for the journey to Jerusalem.
> Luke 9:54 And when His disciples James and John saw *this,* they said, "Lord, do You want us to command fire to come down from heaven and consume them, just as Elijah did?"
> Luke 9:55 But He turned and rebuked them, and said, "You do not know what manner of spirit you are of.

Scripture is clear concerning retaliation and revenge.

> Rom. 12:19 Beloved, do not avenge yourselves, but Rather give place to wrath; for it is written, "Vengeance is Mine, I will repay," says the Lord.
> Rom. 12:20 Therefore "If your enemy is hungry,

> feed him; If he is thirsty, give him a drink; for in so doing you will heap coals of fire on his head."
> Rom. 12:21 Do not be overcome by evil, but overcome evil with good.

How then do we explain what seems to be a wrong attitude on Asaph's part? He asked God to "make them like the whirling dust, like the chaff before the wind." Persecute them, make them afraid, fill their faces with shame! Let them be confounded, troubled, put to shame, and perish!

Asaph was not hating on his enemies. He was not offended for himself, but for the Lord, and that makes all the difference. Throughout his prayer, he was very conscious of the Lord's interests. It was *God's* enemies (vs. 2), those who hated *Him* (vs. 2), who were conspiring together against *His* people (vs. 3) and who were allied together against *Him* (vs. 5) to destroy *His* people (vs. 4).

When the Axis powers were rapidly moving across Europe during World War II, prayer was offered daily by Christians and non-Christians alike for the defeat of Hitler and his hordes. Were they wrong to pray like that? Certainly not, neither were they hating on their enemies. They were humbly pleading for God's mercy and help in what seemed to be an increasingly hopeless situation.

Asking God to do what He alone has the right and responsibility to do—judge the wicked and exact retribution—is cooperating with God and praying in harmony with His will, word, and ways. Moreover, when we turn our enemies over to the Lord and allow Him to take vengeance, it frees us to respond with grace and protects us from anger and bitterness.

Asaph's prayer was in harmony with God's covenant promises in the law of Moses.

> Lev. 26:6 I will give peace in the land, and you shall lie down, and none will make *you* afraid; I will rid the

> land of evil beasts, and the sword will not go through your land.
> Lev. 26:7 You will chase your enemies, and they shall fall by the sword before you.
> Lev. 26:8 Five of you shall chase a hundred, and a hundred of you shall put ten thousand to flight; your enemies shall fall by the sword before you.

The psalmist's prayer also agreed with the Lord's promises to Solomon at the dedication of the temple in Jerusalem.

> 2 Chron. 6:34 "When Your people go out to battle against their enemies, wherever You send them, and when they pray to You toward this city which You have chosen and the temple which I have built for Your name,
> 2 Chron. 6:35 Then hear from heaven their prayer and their supplication, and maintain their cause.

> 2 Chron. 7:12 Then the Lord appeared to Solomon by night, and said to him: "I have heard your prayer, and have chosen this place for Myself as a house of sacrifice.

Asaph's prayer was not prideful or vindictive. It was a prayer of faith and humility, so he appealed to the Lord to mete out justice just as the Scriptures directed. His prayer was in harmony with God's will, God's ways, and God's word.

What can we learn from Asaph's example? Do you understand God's will and His ways well enough to pray in harmony with them?

4-8 The Right Motive

James cautioned us about the importance of motives in prayer.

> James 4:3 You ask and do not receive, because you ask amiss, that you may spend *it* on your pleasures.

Our prayers will be ineffective if our motives are selfish. Concern for self is a powerful motivation, but when it comes to imprecatory prayer, we must be in oneness with the Lord and motivated by the right reasons.

Asaph's motives were clear from the outset. He was concerned about what concerned God—His enemies (vs. 2), His people (vs. 3), His purposes (vs. 4), His person (vs. 5), and His land (vs. 12).

> Ps. 83:2 …*Your* enemies…those who hate *You*...
> Ps. 83:3 …taken crafty counsel against *Your* people …against *Your* sheltered ones.
> Ps. 83:4 …let us *cut them off* from *being* a nation, that *the name of Israel may be remembered no more*."
> Ps. 83:5 …they form a confederacy against *You*:
> Ps. 83:12 …Let us take to ourselves the houses (habitations) of God in possession.

Furthermore, as Asaph closed his prayer, he gave two powerful reasons for God to grant his petitions.

> Ps. 83:16 Fill their faces with shame, that they may seek Your name, O Lord.
> Ps. 83:17 Let them be confounded and dismayed forever; yes, let them be put to shame and perish,
> Ps. 83:18 That they may know that You, whose name alone *is* the LORD, *are* the most high over all the earth.

The psalmist's motives were not fear, panic, self-preservation, revenge, or even the desire to rejoice over his enemies. He wanted *those who do not seek the Lord to seek Him* and *those who do not know the Lord to know Him*. His motivation was the glory of God.

Paul instructed the church at Corinth to pray a bold and unusual petition for one of their members.

> 1 Cor. 5:4 In the name of our Lord Jesus Christ, when you are gathered together, along with my spirit, with the power of our Lord Jesus Christ,

> 1 Cor. 5:5 Deliver such a one to Satan for the destruction of the flesh, that his spirit may be saved in the day of the Lord Jesus.

A similar prayer was doubtless offered by Paul on behalf of two men he referenced in his first letter to Timothy.

> 1 Tim. 1:19 Having faith and a good conscience, which some having rejected, concerning the faith have suffered shipwreck,
> 1 Tim. 1:20 Of whom are Hymenaeus and Alexander, whom I delivered to Satan that they may learn not to blaspheme.

The motive in both cases was not retaliatory but redemptive. Paul was not concerned for himself, his reputation, or his interests but the glory of God, the interests of Christ, and the best interests of those involved. When we pray for the defeat of Satan's agenda for our nation or even the salvation of the lost, our motive must be that Christ would be magnified. If our motive is based in pride, selfishness, fear, personal grievance, revenge, etc., we are asking amiss, and the Lord will not grant our requests.

In His high priestly prayer, Jesus appealed to His Father using a powerful argument based on the same motive.

> John 17:1 Jesus spoke these words, lifted up His eyes to heaven, and said: "Father, the hour has come. Glorify Your Son, that Your Son also may glorify You,

The glory and honor of God is frequently referenced in both testaments and is a fundamental, if not the primary theme of the Bible.

> Ps. 96:1 Oh, sing to the Lord a new song! Sing to the Lord, all the earth.
> Ps. 96:2 Sing to the Lord, bless His name; proclaim the good news of His salvation from day to day.
> Ps. 96:3 Declare His glory among the nations, His wonders among all peoples.

> Ps. 96:4 For the Lord is great and greatly to be praised; He *is* to be feared above all gods.
> Ps. 96:5 For all the gods of the peoples *are* idols, but the Lord made the heavens.

> Isa. 42:8 I *am* the Lord, that *is* My name; and My glory I will not give to another, nor My praise to carved images.

The glory of God is also the highest and purest motive a person can have.

> 1 Cor. 10:31 Therefore, whether you eat or drink, or whatever you do, do all to the glory of God.

Why should we pray for revival and awakening? Why do we want to see change in America? Is it to see the ungodly punished and scoffers put in their place? Is it to get us back to the way America use to be? Is it to escape the suffering and persecution that will likely come if there is not a change of course? Is it to avoid the chaos and hardship that will result if our nation continues its decline? Those motives are primarily self-centered, but there is a higher, purer motive that God always honors. It is His glory—*that those who do not seek the Lord will seek Him* and *those who do not know the Lord will come to know Him.*

Do you want to be an effective intercessor? It will not be easy; it is hard work. Intercessory prayer requires you to meditate in God's Word and learn to think His thoughts. It means listening to God and allowing Him to teach you how to pray. It requires you to study, and struggle, and grow in your prayer life. It often means praying in ways that may feel uncomfortable at first.

Today God is looking for intercessors. He is searching for men and women who will ask like the disciples of old, "Lord, teach us to pray."

- Will you let God teach you to pray boldly?

- Will you learn to give God reasons for granting your requests?

- Will you let Him teach you to discern Satan's strategy?

- Will you purpose to search the Scriptures and pray according to the word of God, the will of God, and the ways of God?

- Do you understand the devil's ultimate objective?

- Will you choose God's glory above everything else?

Can Jesus count on you?

5- A Prayer Guide For America

I exhort first that supplications, prayers, intercessions, and giving of thanks be made for all in authority…1 Tim. 2:1-2

5-1 A Prayer Template

In this final section, you will find a prayer template that has been very meaningful to me in praying for America. It draws from Daniel's prayer, but it also incorporates Asaph's intercession in Psalm 83. Interspersed throughout are additional scripture verses and portions used as praise, confession, petition, etc., with their accompanying references.

Like many others, I have found that praying God's word is the most satisfying way to communicate with Him. It also helps to keep my prayers in harmony with the will and ways of God. Moreover, as you express yourself in the words of Scripture, God will renew your mind and open your understanding of the verses you are praying. Before using the guide, take a moment to read the background Scriptures to better understand and appreciate the significance of each statement. Also, feel free to adapt it to fit your needs.

The prayer guide follows the basic outline of Daniel's intercession (Dan. 9):

- Address and recognition of God (vs. 4).
- Confession of sin (vs. 5-10).
- Acknowledgement of God's discipline (vs. 11-15).
- A plea for mercy and forgiveness (vs. 16-19).

In addition to the features listed above, there are two other kinds of petitions.

- Petitions for those in authority (1 Tim. 2:1-4).
- Imprecatory prayers for God's enemies (Ps. 83:1-18).

5-2 Address And Recognition Of God

Daniel addressed his prayer to the great and awesome (terrible) God, who keeps His covenant and mercy with those who love Him and keep His commandments. In doing so, he reminded himself of some facts about God that actually bolstered his faith and confidence that he would be heard.

In the model prayer, Jesus taught us to address God as "Our Father" because it honors Him as Maker, Protector, and Provider. It also predisposes us to believe He will hear our prayer, based on our experience with earthly fathers who loved and cared for us.

When we appeal to Deity, our address should be related to our request. Daniel and his people had been sternly judged by God and removed from their homeland, so he addressed the Lord as "great and terrible God." He asked the Lord to remember His relationship and promises to Israel, so he addressed Him as the One "who keeps His covenant and mercy with those who love Him and with those who keep His commandments." When we pray, our address should likewise relate to our request.

Other passages are equally appropriate, but I have chosen to use a portion of Psalm 33 because it exalts God's word, works, attributes, creative power, and sovereign rule. In light of the needs we are facing in America, it reminds us of who God is, what He has done, and what He can do. Consequently, the language of Psalm 33 is very appropriate to use in addressing and appealing to the LORD.

****

Almighty God, Maker and Ruler Of Heaven and Earth,

- *Your word is right; and all Your works are done in truth.*
- *You love righteousness and judgment: the earth is full of Your goodness.*
- *By Your word were the heavens made; and all the host of them by the breath of Your mouth.*
- *You gather the waters of the sea together as a heap: You lay up the depth in storehouses.*
- *Let all the earth fear You, O LORD: let all the inhabitants of the world stand in awe.*
- *For You spoke, and it was done; You commanded, and it stood fast.*
- *O LORD, You bring the counsel of the nations to naught: You make the devices of the people of none effect.*
- *Your counsel, O LORD, stands forever, the thoughts of Your heart to all generations (Ps. 33:5-11).*

5-3 Confession Of Sin

Confession of sin is fully agreeing with God in His assessment of our wrong behavior.

> 1 John 1:8 If we say that we have no sin, we deceive ourselves, and the truth is not in us.

> 1 John 1:9 If we confess our sins, He is faithful and just to forgive us *our* sins and to cleanse us from all unrighteousness.

In this case, it is our *corporate* wrongdoing that needs to be acknowledged and brought to the light. In your personal walk with the Lord, you may be completely innocent, but as a nation, America has greatly offended the LORD.

Blanket confession is not nearly as effective as specific confession, so it is helpful to identify and confess specific ways we have departed from the Lord.

****

King, Master, and Governor of the nations,

We have sinned, committed iniquity, done wickedly, and rebelled by...

- *Removing prayer and Bible reading from our homes, schools, and public life (Deut. 6:7);*
- *Refusing to train our children in the way they should go and indoctrinating them with the lies of atheism and evolution (Deut. 6:6-7: Ps. 14:1);*
- *Not respecting Your Day and forsaking Your houses of worship in the land (Ex. 20:8; Heb. 10:25);*
- *Rejecting Biblical authority and moral absolutes and embracing situational ethics and relativism (Ex. 20:2-17);*
- *Dishonoring You by dishonoring Your only Son, Jesus, and equating all religions (John 5:22-23; 14:6; Deut. 7:5);*
- *Worshipping and serving the creature rather than You, our Creator (Rom. 1:25);*
- *Defiling ourselves and wasting time through entertainment that promotes crudeness, sensuality, promiscuity, violence, revenge, cruelty, disrespect for authority, profanity, perversion, and blasphemy (Eph. 5:16; Phil. 4:8);*
- *Oppressing and exploiting the poor and needy (Pro. 14:21);*
- *Trafficking in drugs, alcohol, and the souls of men, women, and children (Rev. 9:21; Ex. 21:16);*

- *Shedding innocent blood and harvesting their body parts for sale (Ps. 106:37-38);*
- *Normalizing and celebrating sexual immorality—fornication, adultery, divorce, pornography, prostitution, homosexuality, transgender-ism, etc., (1 Thess. 4:3-5);*
- *Legalizing gambling and redefining marriage by statute (Col. 3:5; Ps. 94:20).*

Moreover, we have refused to heed Your correction by...

- *Ignoring the still small voice of Your Spirit speaking in our hearts (1 Kings 19:11-13);*
- *Refusing to listen to Your preachers and prophets (Dan. 9:6);*
- *Disregarding Your reproofs of life—conflicts in health, finances, relationships, jobs, etc. (Pro. 15:31);*
- *Refusing to humble our proud hearts despite increasing disasters (Isa. 9:13).*

5- 4 Acknowledgement Of God's Discipline

A fundamental principle of life is cause and effect. It is woven into the fabric of creation. If you have a cause, there must be an effect. If you have an effect, something must have caused it. If you have an infinitely complex and ordered universe (effect), you must have an infinitely wise and powerful universe Maker (cause).

A corollary in terms of human behavior is "actions have consequences."

> Gal. 6:7 Do not be deceived, God is not mocked; for whatever a man sows, that he will also reap.

To be rightly related to God, we must acknowledge and cooperate with Him in what He is doing. To join Him in His work of repentance, we must acknowledge our sin (action) and His discipline (consequence). To refuse to acknowledge this fundamental principle is to reject our Creator and His design of the world. It is to willingly choose a world of fantasy instead of reality.

****

God Most High and Judge Of All The Earth,

- *Righteousness belongs to You, but shame belongs to us and our leaders because we have not obeyed Your commandments.*
- *Therefore You have brought upon us a great evil.*
- *And though judgment has come, still we have not repented and turned from our iniquities and understood Your truth.*
- *Therefore, You have watched over the evil and brought it upon us: for You are righteous in all Your works (Dan. 9:7-14).*

We have walked contrary to You and You have walked contrary to us (Lev. 26:41). You have judged us through...

- *The breakdown of marriage and family life—absentee fathers, career-minded mothers, and prodigal children; a growing incidence of single parent families, divorce, cohabitation and same sex unions; child neglect and abuse; role reversals in our homes and gender confusion among our children; an increasing incidence of teen pregnancies and children born outside of marriage; and a declining birth rate among Christians;*
- *Failing schools that impart knowledge without the fear of God;*
- *Epidemic drug abuse, STD's, and suicide;*
- *Addictions, phobias, and excesses of all kinds (O.C.D., panic attacks, gluttony, anorexia, bulimia, hoarding, etc.);*
- *Crime, mayhem, and anarchy in our streets;*
- *Environmental pollution, homelessness, and a growing demographic dependent on governmental assistance;*
- *Needless illness and disease overwhelming our health care system;*
- *Frivolous lawsuits, injustice in our courts, and judicial activism;*

- *Oppressive taxation to support wasteful and immoral spending;*
- *A staggering national debt, economic uncertainty, and financial calamities;*
- *Growing government control of our private lives;*
- *Corrupt and deceitful politicians who enrich themselves rather than serve their constituents;*
- *Illegal immigration and foreigners buying up our land;*
- *Increasing disasters of storm, fire, flood, earthquake, pestilence, and terror;*
- *Anxiety, panic, and fearfulness about the future (pandemics, climate change, financial collapse, nuclear war, etc.);*
- *Giving us leaders who hate Christ and Judeo-Christian values;*
- *Persecution of Christians and Jews;*

We have refused to love the truth and delighted in unrighteousness, so You have sent us strong delusion that we should believe the lie (2 Thess. 2:11-12).

5-5 A Plea For Mercy And Forgiveness

God is not impressed with human goodness or achievement.

> Ps. 62:9 Surely men of low degree *are* a vapor, men of high degree *are* a lie; if they are weighed on the scales, they *are* altogether *lighter* than vapor.

The best we have to offer God—our righteousness—is like filthy rags in His sight.

> Isa. 64:6 But we are all like an unclean *thing*, and all our righteousnesses *are* like filthy rags; we all fade as a leaf, and our iniquities, like the wind, have taken us away.

When we try to make up for our sin with good deeds, we insult God's holiness and ignore a fundamental truth about how we must relate to God.

The Lord is infinitely righteous, and He rewards every person according to his works.

> Ps. 62:12 Also to You, O Lord, *belongs* mercy; for You render to each one according to his work.

Since there is none righteous and the best we can offer God is no better than filthy rags, forgiveness is only possible on the basis of His mercy.

> Lam. 3:22 Through the Lord's mercies we are not consumed, because His compassions fail not.

In mercy, God gives us what we need rather than what we deserve. Once we understand this truth, we realize like Daniel that our plea for forgiveness must be based on the mercy of God and not our human merit.

****

Only true God, Father of our Lord Jesus Christ,

- *Remember Your covenant in the blood of Jesus (Ps. 74:20; Mt. 26:28).*
- *Awaken Your saints, and stir Your remnant; let judgment begin at the house of God (Hag. 1:14; 1 Pet. 4:17).*
- *Forgive our sins, and the iniquities of our fathers (rebellion, deceit, covetousness, exploitation, murder, slavery, oppression of the poor, shedding innocent blood, and perversion (Lev. 26:40-45; Dan. 9:8-16).*
- *Revive Your church, and awaken America (Jer. 18:7-8).*

In Jesus' name, hear our united prayer, but not because of our righteousness, for all our righteousness is as filthy rags (Dan. 9:18a; Isa. 64:6).

- *Not that we may continue our selfish pursuit of the American dream (Luke 16:25-26),*

- *Not that we may walk in pride and rebellion. (Eze. 16:49a),*
- *Not that we may live in security, ease and abundance, ignoring the needs of others (Eze. 16:49b).*
- *Not that we may arrogantly commit abomination until You come and take us away (Eze. 16:50).*

But hear our prayer because of Your great mercy (Dan. 9:18b)...

- *That believers may lead a quiet and peaceable life in all godliness and honesty (1 Tim. 2:2b);*
- *That we may train up our children in the way they should go (Pro. 22:6);*
- *That we may freely worship You, promote Biblical values, proclaim Christ, and make disciples (Mt. 5:13; Mt. 28:19-20);*
- *That Christians may sacrificially support missions and fulfill the Great Commission (Phil. 4:15-18; Mt. 28:19-20);*
- *That America may uphold the sanctity of life, marriage, and family as You ordained them (Ex. 20:13; Eph. 5:22-25);*
- *That America may be a refuge for the oppressed and promote truth, righteousness, and freedom in the world (Mt. 5:14-16);*
- *That America may be a blessing to Israel (Gen. 12:3);*
- *That all may know that this is Your hand, that You have done it (Ps. 109:26-27).*

5-6 Petitions For Those In Authority

As citizens of America, we are commanded to render to governmental rulers honor and obedience. Whether King, dictator, or elected leader, all authorities are ordained by God. To disrespect or disobey them is to disrespect the Lord who put them in their position.

> Rom. 13:1 <u>Let every soul be subject</u> to the governing authorities. For t<u>here is no authority except from God</u>, and <u>the authorities that exist are appointed by God</u>.

> Rom. 13:2 Therefore whoever resists the authority resists the ordinance of God, and those who resist will bring judgment on themselves.

The only time a Christian may engage in civil disobedience is when to obey an authority requires that we disobey Christ. The classic example of appropriate civil disobedience is when the disciples were commanded by the Jewish leaders not to preach and teach in Jesus' name. Note their response.

> Acts 4:18 So they called them and commanded them not to speak at all nor teach in the name of Jesus.
> Acts 4:19 But Peter and John answered and said to them, "Whether it is right in the sight of God to listen to you more than to God, you judge.
> Acts 4:20 For we cannot but speak the things which we have seen and heard."

Part of honoring and respecting leaders is praying regularly for them as Scripture commands.

> 1 Tim. 2:1 Therefore I exhort first of all that supplications, prayers, intercessions, *and* giving of thanks be made for all men,
> 1 Tim. 2:2 For kings and all who are in authority, that we may lead a quiet and peaceable life in all godliness and reverence.

In addition to elected leaders, there are other authorities and those in unelected positions of influence who powerfully impact our lives for good or evil. It is important that we not overlook them in our daily intercession.

****

King Of Nations, True and Living God,

- *Thank You for shedding Your grace on America—for the beauty and bounty of our land, for our Christian heritage, our form of government, and our freedom (Ps. 33:12).*

- *Thank You for establishing, preserving, and prospering this great nation for many generations (Ps. 127:1).*
- *Have mercy on America, restore the ancient landmarks, and rebuild the foundations of many generations (Pro. 22:28; Isa. 55:12).*
- *Raise up a standard against the flood of evil that threatens our national existence (Isa. 59:19).*
- *By Your Spirit, wash, sanctify, and justify our president and his family in the name of Jesus (1 Cor. 6:11).*
- *Protect and empower him to accomplish the work You have given him to do (Isa. 45:1-6).*
- *Preserve him from violent men, who plan evil things in their hearts and continually gather together for war (Ps. 140:1-2).*
- *Give us judges and leaders who fear You and tremble at Your word (Isa. 66:2).*
- *Give us leaders who will bless Israel and support their right to independence and sovereignty in the land You gave to Abraham, Isaac, and Jacob (Gen. 12:3; 17:8).*
- *Raise up leaders who will balance the federal budget; restore the fear of God as the foundation of education; appoint constitutionally conservative Supreme Court Justices and lower court judges; end abortion on demand by revoking Roe v Wade; restore the Biblical definition of marriage and family; end the waste and abuse of government programs; protect religious freedom and promote in every area of our national life the values that helped foster America's greatness (Pro. 14:34).*
- *Give us leaders who will stand for Biblical morality; marriage and family life as you ordained it; the sanctity of life; character centered education; religious liberty; a Biblical work ethic; fiscal responsibility; free enterprise; property rights; freedom of conscience and speech; the rule of law; equality and justice for all (Ps. 101:1-8; Pro. 16:12).*
- *Confound those in leadership and public life who refuse to call upon Your name, but lay up of Your goodness for those who trust in You before the sons of men (Jer. 10:25; Ps. 31:19).*

5-7 Prayer For God's Enemies

This kind of prayer may seem harsh at first, but consider the following passages. When the enemies of the Jews opposed the rebuilding of the wall of Jerusalem, Nehemiah prayed,

> Neh. 4:4 Hear, O our God, for we are despised; turn their reproach on their own heads, and give them as plunder to a land of captivity!
> Neh. 4:5 Do not cover their iniquity, and do not let their sin be blotted out from before You; for they have provoked *You* to anger before the builders.

Jesus taught and encouraged imprecatory prayer in the parable of the unjust judge.

> Luke 18:6 Then the Lord said, "Hear what the unjust judge said.
> Luke 18:7 And shall God not avenge His own elect who cry out day and night to Him, though He bears long with them?
> Luke 18:8 I tell you that He will avenge them speedily…"

Paul used this kind of prayer in reference to those who opposed his ministry.

> 2 Tim. 4:14 Alexander the coppersmith did me much harm. May the Lord repay him according to his works.

The souls under the altar in heaven who were slain for the word of God and for their testimony cry out to God for vengeance.

> Rev. 6:10 And they cried with a loud voice, saying, "How long, O Lord, holy and true, until You judge and avenge our blood on those who dwell on the earth?"

When we pray, we join God in what He is doing. Sometimes, His work is saving, reviving, and restoring. However, His work also involves judgment as with the Babylonian captivity.

> Hab. 1:5 "Look among the nations and watch—be utterly astounded! For *I will* work a work in your days *which* you would not believe, though it were told *you*.
> Hab. 1:6 For indeed I am raising up the Chaldeans, a bitter and hasty nation which marches through the breadth of the earth, to possess dwelling places *that are* not theirs.

Oneness is agreement and identification with God, even when we do not understand or desire His will. Moreover, oneness is the key to authority in prayer, and "the deeper the oneness, the greater the authority" (T. W. Hunt).

> 1 John 5:14 Now this is the confidence that we have in Him, that if we ask anything according to His will, He hears us.
> 1 John 5:15 And if we know that He hears us, whatever we ask, we know that we have the petitions that we have asked of Him.

****

Just and Righteous King, LORD Of Hosts,

- *Do not keep silent! Do not hold Your peace, and do not be still!*
- *For behold, Your enemies make a tumult; And those who hate You have lifted up their head.*
- *They have taken crafty counsel against Your people, and consulted together against Your saints.*
- *They say, "Come, and let us silence their voice, that the name of Jesus may be remembered no more."*
- *They consult together with one consent: Liberal activists in the justice system, business, politics, education, religion, the media, and entertainment have formed a confederacy against You:*
- *They denounce You, defy You, and say, "There is no God" and "With our tongue we will prevail; our lips are our own; who is lord over us?" (Ps. 14:1; Ps. 12:3-4).*
- *O my God, make them like the whirling dust, like the chaff before the wind!*

- *Pursue them with Your tempest, and frighten them with Your storm.*
- *Fill their faces with shame, that they may seek Your name, O Lord (Ps. 83:1-18).*
- *Put them in fear, O Lord, that they may know themselves to be but men (Ps. 9:20).*
- *Do not grant the desires of the wicked; do not further his wicked schemes lest they exalt themselves (Ps. 140:8).*
- *Bring upon the wicked their own iniquity, and cut them off in their own wickedness (Ps. 94:23).*
- *Bring their counsel to nothing: make their schemes of none effect (Ps. 33:10).*
- *Stop the mouths of liars, and let not an evil speaker be established in the earth (Ps. 31:18; 140:11).*
- *Give them according to their deeds, and according to the wickedness of their endeavors; give them according to the work of their hands; render to them what they deserve (Ps. 28:4).*
- *Since they regard not Your works, O LORD, nor the operation of Your hands, break them down and do not build them up (Ps. 28:5).*
- *Let them be confounded and dismayed; yes, let them be put to shame, that they may know that You, whose name alone is the LORD, are the Most High over all the earth (Ps. 83:17-18).*

Sovereign Master, Ruler of Heaven and Earth,

- *As the clay is in the potter's hand, so are we in Your hand.*
- *You uproot, pull down, and destroy nations that forget You, but You spare, plant and build nations that turn from their evil (Jer. 18:5-11).*
- *Turn us, O LORD God of hosts; incline our hearts to good and not to evil (Ps. 141:4).*
- *Quicken us, and we will call upon Your name (Ps. 80:18).*
- *Cause Your face to shine, and we shall be saved (Ps. 80: 19)!*
- *Stay Your hand of judgment; spare America (Jer. 18:7-8).*
- *For Jesus' sake, revive Your church, and send healing to our nation while there's still time (Isa. 55:6).*

6- Conclusion: Buying Time

Because he has humbled himself before Me, I will not bring the calamity in his days…1 Kings 21:29

In Israel's entire history, there was never a king as wicked as Ahab with his evil consort, Jezebel.

> 1 Kings 16:30 Now Ahab the son of Omri did evil in the sight of the Lord, more than all who *were* before him.
> 1 Kings 16:31 And it came to pass, as though it had been a trivial thing for him to walk in the sins of Jeroboam the son of Nebat, that he took as wife Jezebel the daughter of Ethbaal, king of the Sidonians; and he went and served Baal and worshiped him.
> 1 Kings 16:32 Then he set up an altar for Baal in the temple of Baal, which he had built in Samaria.
> 1 Kings 16:33 And Ahab made a wooden image. Ahab did more to provoke the Lord God of Israel to anger than all the kings of Israel who were before him.

His unparalleled reign of wickedness lasted twenty-two long years, but finally, the Lord sent Elijah, the Tishbite, to pronounce judgment on Ahab and his family. It was a grievous rebuke, reflecting the grief he had caused the Lord.

> 1 Kings 21:21 'Behold, I will bring calamity on you. I will take away your posterity, and will cut off from Ahab every male in Israel, both bond and free.
> 1 Kings 21:22 I will make your house like the house of Jeroboam the son of Nebat, and like the house of Baasha the son of Ahijah, because of the provocation with which you have provoked *Me* to anger, and made Israel sin.'
> 1 Kings 21:23 And concerning Jezebel the Lord also spoke, saying, 'The dogs shall eat Jezebel by the wall of Jezreel.'
> 1 Kings 21:24 The dogs shall eat whoever belongs to Ahab and dies in the city, and the birds of the air shall eat whoever dies in the field."

When Ahab heard the words of Elijah, he did the unexpected, and God showed mercy to the contrite King. Ahab tore his clothing, lay in sackcloth, fasted, and went about mourning. Then the word of the Lord came to Elijah.

> 1 Kings 21:29 "See how Ahab has humbled himself before Me? Because he has humbled himself before Me, I will not bring the calamity in his days. In the days of his son I will bring the calamity on his house."

Judgment could not be averted, but it was delayed. God gave Ahab and his people a reprieve; He postponed the inevitable because Ahab humbled himself.

Given our past offenses, the increasing lawlessness of our society, and the current contempt of all things Christian, I do not believe America can escape the ultimate judgment of God. Without a sweeping revival that changes the spiritual and moral atmosphere of our nation, destruction is unavoidable. However, I do believe we can postpone the inevitable; we can buy some time if we earnestly seek the Lord.

"Mercy drops" will not suffice. We need "showers of blessings." In short, we need a revival of Biblical proportions. God has done it in the past, and He can do it again. We cannot manufacture revival or spiritual awakening, but we can meet God's conditions and hope in His mercy. While there's still time, will you believe God and claim His promises?

Interest in intercessory prayer is growing. Calls from Christian leaders to repentance and prayer are increasing. God is moving among His people. The Holy Spirit is speaking to the churches. Jesus is calling us to seek His face. May God give us grace to declare with the psalmist,

> Ps. 27:7 Hear, O Lord, *when* I cry with my voice! Have mercy also upon me, and answer me.
> Ps. 27:8 *When You said,* "Seek My face," My heart said to You, "Your face, O Lord, I will seek."

SCRIPTURE INDEX

1- A NATION IN NEED OF HEALING

2- DISASTERS: WHY?

3- STAND IN THE GAP

Pg. 36 - Dan. 9:4; Eze. 14:13-14
Pg. 37 - Heb. 9:18-20
Pg. 38 - Dan. 9:5-6; 9:9-10; 9:8; 9:11-12
Pg. 39 - Dan. 9:13; 9:7; 9:16
Pg. 40 - Rev. 2:4-5; Dan. 9:16-19
Pg. 41 - Dan. 9:7, 14; 1 John 1:10
Pg. 42 - Lev. 26:40-41
Pg. 43 - Ex. 32:12-13; John 17:1; Dan. 9:4
Pg. 44 - Dan. 9:7, 14; 9:4, 9, 18; 9:15; 9:17-19
Pg. 45 - Ps. 106:37-40
Pg. 46 - Dan. 9:18; Ps. 86:5
Pg. 47 - Lev. 26:39; 26:40-41; Ps. 12:1
Pg. 48 - Jer. 18:7-8
Pg. 49 - Jonah 3:4; 3:10; Jer. 18:11

4- WARFARE PRAYING

Pg. 52 - Luke 24:44; 2 Tim. 3:16-17; Ps. 5:10; 79:6-7
Pg. 53 - Ps. 83:1
Pg. 54 - Acts 4:24-30; John 14:12-14
Pg. 55 - John 15:7; Acts 1:8; Ps. 83:2-5
Pg. 56 - Job 9:32-33
Pg. 57 - Ps. 83:2-5
Pg. 58 - 2 Cor. 2:11; Ps. 83:6-8
Pg. 60 - Rom. 5:10; Ps. 83:9-11; Judges 4:14-16
Pg. 61 - Judges 7:25; 8:21
Pg. 63 - Ps. 140:4, 8-9, 11; 83:12; Isa. 14:13-14
Pg. 64 - Eph. 2:1-2; Luke 13:34
Pg. 65 – Luke 19:41-44; 1 Cor. 3:16-17; Rev. 2:14, 20
Pg. 66 - 2 Thess. 2:3-4; Rev. 20:7-9
Pg. 67 - Ps. 83:13-17; Luke 9:53-55; Rom. 12:19-21
Pg. 68 - Lev. 26:6-8
Pg. 69 - 2 Chron. 6:34-35; 7:12; James 4:3
Pg. 70 - Ps. 83:16-18; 1 Cor. 5:4-5
Pg. 71 - 1 Tim. 1:19-20; John 17:1; Ps. 96:1-5
Pg. 72 - Isa. 42:8; 1 Cor. 10:31

5- A GUIDE TO PRAYING FOR AMERICA

Pg. 76 - 1 John 1:8-9
Pg. 78 - Gal. 6:7
Pg. 80 - Ps. 62:9; Isa. 64:6
Pg. 81 - Isa. 62:12; Lam. 3:22
Pg. 82 - Rom. 13:1-2
Pg. 83 - Acts 4:18-20; 1 Tim. 2:1-2
Pg. 85 - Neh. 4:4-5; Luke 18:6-8; 2 Tim. 4:14; Rev. 6:10
Pg. 86 - Hab. 1:5-6; 1 John 5:14-15

6- CONCLUSION: BUYING TIME

Pg. 88 - 1 Kings 16:30-33
Pg. 89 - 1 Kings 21:21-24; 21:29
Pg. 90 - Ps. 27:7-8

ABOUT THE AUTHOR

Joel R. Stroud is a Southern Baptist pastor, living in Lyon, MS where he has served Lyon Baptist Church since August of 1989. His spiritual upbringing was in rural churches of Mississippi, Alabama, Georgia, and Florida, served by his father, Daniel W. Stroud, Sr., a bi-vocational pastor and educator. In 1975 while teaching Bible and coaching in Memphis, TN, he met and married his wife and best friend, Sheri Ricks Stroud. They have one son, Joel Seth, a singer, songwriter, and worship leader, living nearby in Clarksdale with his wife and family. Pastor Stroud is a graduate of Delta State University and New Orleans Baptist Theological Seminary. Before coming to Lyon, he served for three and a half years as pastor of Silver Springs Baptist Church near Progress, MS.

Other works by the author:

Thinking His Thoughts: Renewing Your Mind Through Daily Meditation In The Psalms & Proverbs; 299 pg.

Rightly Related: Going Deeper In Your Relationship With Jesus; 109 pg.

It's All Good: Praying In Harmony With God's Purposes In Suffering; 80 pg.

Discipleship According To Jesus: A Concise Survey Of The Requirements And Implications Of Discipleship; 24 pg.

No Greater Work: Essays On Effective Prayer; 54 pg.

Contact the author at joelrstroud@gmail.com

Made in the USA
Columbia, SC
22 June 2020

10785353R00059